Propaganda of the Deed

Bradley Hall

Published by Bradley Hall, 2024.

Table of Contents

Disclaimer

A NECESSARY DISCLAIMER: Understanding Without Endorsing

This book, *Propaganda of the Deed: A Manifesto of Action*, is an exploration of the concept of propaganda of the deed as a historical, philosophical, and practical phenomenon. It seeks to educate and provoke thought about the ways individuals and groups have attempted to inspire social and political change through symbolic action. However, it is of the utmost importance to clarify that this book does not condone, endorse, or encourage illegal, unethical, or violent actions of any kind.

Propaganda of the deed encompasses a wide range of tactics, some of which include actions that have caused harm, destruction, and even loss of life. While this book discusses these events for the sake of understanding their historical and cultural impact, such mention does not equate to support or approval.

Understanding Does Not Equal Approval

History is complex, and the human capacity for both great good and great harm is evident in the examples presented in this book. Actions such as self-immolation, assassination, bombings, property destruction, and other extreme forms of direct action are discussed here not to glorify them but to analyze their motives, impacts, and outcomes. In some cases, these actions have catalyzed meaningful change; in others, they have caused devastating consequences and unintended harm.

This book aims to illuminate the context, strategies, and ethics surrounding propaganda of the deed to encourage critical thinking and responsible action. At no point should the discussion of historical or theoretical examples be interpreted as a call to imitate or replicate such acts.

Extreme Actions Discussed in This Book

To ensure absolute clarity, the following is a non-exhaustive list of extreme forms of propaganda of the deed discussed within these pages. While these actions are explored in a historical or analytical context, we unequivocally state that we do not condone, encourage, or support:

- **Self-immolation**: The act of setting oneself on fire as a form of protest. While acts like these have been powerful symbols in certain historical contexts, they are inherently dangerous and devastating.

- **Assassination**: The targeted killing of individuals to send a political message, such as the murder of Alexander II or other political leaders.

- **Bombings**: Attacks on infrastructure or gatherings intended to disrupt, provoke, or terrorize.

- **Violence against individuals**: Physical harm or intimidation directed at people to achieve political goals.

- **Acts of terrorism**: Actions intended to cause widespread fear or harm to civilians, often misusing the principles of propaganda of the deed for destructive purposes.

- **Vandalism and property destruction**: Actions that cause material damage, even when aimed at symbolic targets.

- **Hunger strikes leading to severe harm**: Acts of personal sacrifice that risk severe physical consequences.

- **Environmental sabotage**: Actions such as arson or destruction of equipment, even in the name of protecting natural resources.

- **Cyberattacks**: Digital hacking that disrupts systems, steals information, or causes harm to organizations or individuals.

While these actions are documented and analyzed, their inclusion is intended solely for educational and analytical purposes. This book neither glorifies nor justifies these actions.

The Importance of Ethical Action

Throughout this book, we emphasize the importance of ethical considerations in any action undertaken in the name of change. Propaganda of the deed is most powerful when it aligns with principles of justice, compassion, and responsibility. Actions that harm innocent individuals, destroy lives, or sow chaos are counterproductive to the goal of building a better, more equitable world.

When reading this book, it is crucial to approach its contents with a discerning mind. Understand the broader context of these deeds, but also recognize that history is filled with lessons about what *not* to do.

A Warning to Readers

If you are considering taking action inspired by the ideas in this book, we urge you to pause and reflect. Ask yourself:

- Is this action ethical?

- Could it cause harm to others, directly or indirectly?

- Are there nonviolent or legal ways to achieve the same goal?

- Am I prepared for the consequences, including legal repercussions?

The decisions you make are your own, and the responsibility for your actions lies solely with you. Neither the author nor the publisher assumes responsibility for any actions taken by readers based on the content of this book.

Encouraging Responsible Activism

This book is ultimately a call for thoughtful, principled action that respects human life and dignity. Many examples of propaganda of the deed, particularly those rooted in nonviolence and civil disobedience, demonstrate how bold, symbolic acts can inspire change without causing harm. This is the legacy we hope readers will take to heart.

If you are inspired to act, consider methods that:

- Align with ethical principles.

- Preserve human life and well-being.

- Build community and solidarity.

- Create positive, sustainable change.

- Stay within the bounds of the law wherever possible.

Legal Notice

This book is a work of analysis and commentary. It is not a guide or instruction manual for engaging in acts of propaganda of the deed or any other form of direct action. The author and publisher disclaim any liability for actions taken by readers. By purchasing or reading this book, you acknowledge that you are solely responsible for your interpretations and actions.

This disclaimer is intended to protect the integrity of the book's purpose: to educate, to provoke thought, and to inspire ethical, informed activism. It is not, and should never be interpreted as, an endorsement or incitement of illegal or harmful behavior.

Closing Thoughts

The world is in desperate need of change, but that change must come from a place of justice, compassion, and responsibility. The actions you take in pursuit of a better world must reflect the values you hope to instill. While this book explores the full spectrum of propaganda of the deed, it is up to you, the reader, to choose your path wisely.

History may be written by the bold, but the future belongs to those who act with integrity.

Introduction

The world has always been on fire.

If you squint at history—strip away the dates, the names, the costumes—it looks like a repeating loop of the same story. Somewhere, a tyrant sharpens their sword, counts their gold, or draws their borders. Somewhere else, a farmer, a teacher, or a mother finally says, *No more.*

The flames leap higher.

This book is about those moments when ordinary people throw water on the fire—or, sometimes, gasoline. It's about actions so bold, so defiant, so impossible to ignore that they shake the very ground beneath our feet. It's about people who said, *Enough is enough,* and chose to do something rather than wait for someone else to do it for them.

This is the story of *propaganda of the deed.*

What Is Propaganda of the Deed?

If the phrase sounds theatrical, it's because it is. Propaganda of the deed isn't just action—it's action with a megaphone. It's the kind of action that screams louder than a thousand speeches, grabs you by the collar, and demands, *Pay attention.*

The concept has roots in anarchist philosophy, where the idea was that one well-placed act—an assassination, a strike, a bombing—could light a spark big enough to ignite a revolution. Over time, the idea has evolved, splintered, and adapted. Now, it encompasses a broad spectrum of tactics, from dramatic acts of protest to devastating acts of violence.

What ties them all together is the intent: to send a message.

But here's the thing: propaganda of the deed isn't just a history lesson or a philosophical puzzle. It's a toolkit. A matchbook, handed down through time.

Why Write This Book Now?

Let's not sugarcoat it: the world is a mess.

The ice caps are melting, the rich are getting richer, and injustice is practically baked into the systems that run our lives. Turn on the news—or open Twitter (or X)—and it feels like the walls are closing in. The question isn't, *Should we act?* It's, *Why haven't we acted already?*

But acting isn't easy.

The forces that hold power want you to feel small. They want you to believe that no matter what you do, it won't matter. That the machine is too big, too strong, and too inevitable to fight.

They're lying.

This book is a reminder that deeds *do* matter. They always have. It's a guide to understanding what makes certain actions effective, why some succeed and others fail, and how you can wield the same tools that countless others have used to challenge power and inspire change.

What This Book Is—and Isn't

Let's be clear: this isn't a "how-to" manual for blowing up pipelines or overthrowing governments. If that's what you're looking for, close this book now.

What this book *is* is a map. It will take you from the theoretical to the practical, from the streets of 19th-century Paris to the digital battlegrounds of the 21st century. Along the way, you'll meet anarchists, suffragettes, environmentalists, and revolutionaries. Some of them succeeded beyond their wildest dreams. Some of them failed spectacularly. All of them have something to teach us.

You'll also learn what it takes to plan and execute an action—ethically, strategically, and responsibly. You'll learn to assess risks, craft messages, and navigate the murky waters of backlash and criticism. Most importantly, you'll learn that you *can* make a difference, no matter how daunting the odds.

A Word of Warning

Propaganda of the deed is not for the faint of heart.

It will not make you rich, popular, or comfortable. It will not solve all your problems or fix the world overnight. It is messy, dangerous, and unpredictable.

But it's also necessary.

Because history doesn't change on its own. It changes when people like you decide to stop waiting, stop hoping, and start doing.

The Fire in Your Hands

If you've made it this far, something inside you is already burning. Maybe it's anger at the state of the world. Maybe it's a quiet sense of injustice you've carried for years. Or maybe it's just the feeling that you were meant to do something bigger, something that matters.

Whatever it is, hold onto it. Nurture it. Because that fire, no matter how small, is where every revolution begins.

This book isn't going to save the world.

But maybe you will.

Chapter 1: What Is Propaganda of the Deed?

———

People don't listen. Not really. They nod and hum, make agreeable noises, maybe even look you in the eye when you're trying to tell them something important. But it's in one ear and out the other. That's human nature. We're distracted, lazy, or maybe just scared of what it means to actually hear someone else's truth.

Now, imagine you're living in the 19th century, and you're not just trying to tell someone your truth—you're trying to shout it into the face of a machine that grinds people into dust. The machine is called "the system" or "the establishment" or "the status quo," and it has a million different gears, each sharper than the last: kings and emperors, police and soldiers, landlords and factory owners.

Words won't cut it, not alone. Speeches can get lost in the din, pamphlets can be burned, and polite protests can be crushed under the boots of riot squads. So what do you do when you're desperate, angry, and convinced that your message needs to be heard?

You act.

That's the beating heart of *propaganda of the deed*: the idea that an act can be louder than a thousand words, that a single strike, dramatic and impossible to ignore, can shake the pillars of power. But it's not just about violence—though there's plenty of that in its bloody history. It's about symbolism. It's about doing something that makes people stop, gasp, and think, "What the hell just happened?" It's about waking them up.

Propaganda of the deed isn't for the faint-hearted. It's a concept born in back rooms thick with smoke and whispered conspiracy, in the fiery rhetoric of anarchists and revolutionaries. It's as dangerous as dynamite and just as unpredictable. But let's not get ahead of ourselves. To understand what it really is, we need to take a little trip back in time.

A Fire in the Belly

The phrase "propaganda of the deed" first popped up in the late 19th century, a time when Europe was a powder keg of political unrest. This was an age of kings and czars, of factory whistles and child labor, of empires stretching their claws into every corner of the globe. The Industrial Revolution had made a few men unimaginably wealthy, but for most, life was cheap, nasty, and short.

In this cauldron of inequality, a movement began to brew: anarchism. Forget for a moment what you think you know about anarchists—the black masks, the Molotov cocktails, the punk rock aesthetic. Back then, anarchists were philosophers, dreamers, and schemers who believed in tearing down oppressive systems and building a world without rulers.

One of these dreamers was a guy named Mikhail Bakunin, a Russian revolutionary who had a knack for stirring the pot.

Bakunin believed that action—bold, daring, and public—could spark revolutions. "The passion for destruction is a creative passion," he wrote, and he wasn't just talking about breaking windows. He meant tearing apart the structures that kept people in chains.

Another anarchist, Carlo Pisacane, took the idea a step further. Pisacane, an Italian revolutionary, argued that words and theories weren't enough to inspire the masses. You needed deeds—dramatic, unforgettable acts—to show people what was possible. He believed that one act of courage could do more to ignite a revolution than a hundred pamphlets.

And so, the idea of propaganda of the deed was born. It wasn't about violence for its own sake. It wasn't nihilism. It was about sending a message so powerful that it couldn't be ignored.

When Words Aren't Enough

Here's the thing about words: they're fragile. You can write the most eloquent argument for justice, pour your heart and soul into it, and it still might not make a dent. People are creatures of habit. They're stuck in their routines, their biases, their blinders.

But a deed—a bold, shocking, unforgettable deed—can cut through all that.

Take, for example, the assassination of Tsar Alexander II of Russia in 1881. The Narodnaya Volya (that's "The People's Will" in English) were a group of radical revolutionaries who believed the only way to topple the Russian autocracy was to strike at its heart. They spent months plotting, smuggling explosives, and outwitting the tsar's secret police. When they finally succeeded in killing him, it was like a thunderclap.

The assassination didn't bring down the Russian Empire, but it sent a message: no one is untouchable. It was a symbolic act, meant to inspire others to rise up against tyranny.

This is the essence of propaganda of the deed: it's not just about the act itself. It's about what the act represents. It's a spark, a provocation, a dare. It says, "Look at what we're willing to do. What are *you* going to do about it?"

A Double-Edged Sword

Now, before we go romanticizing this idea, let's be clear: propaganda of the deed is a dangerous game. It's unpredictable, messy, and often tragic. For every revolutionary act that inspires change, there's another that backfires spectacularly.

The Haymarket Affair of 1886 is a perfect example. It started as a peaceful rally for workers' rights in Chicago, part of the growing labor movement. But when someone threw a bomb into the crowd, killing several police officers, the event spiraled into chaos. Eight anarchists were arrested, and though there was no evidence tying them to the bombing, they were convicted in a sham trial. Four were executed.

The Haymarket bombing became a rallying cry for labor activists around the world, but it also led to a brutal crackdown on anarchists and leftist movements in the United States. That's the gamble with propaganda of the deed: it can inspire, but it can also provoke fear, repression, and backlash.

Deeds, Not Words

One of the reasons propaganda of the deed has such a hold on the imagination is because it taps into something primal. Words are abstract; deeds are concrete. A speech might make you think, but a dramatic act makes you *feel*.

This is why activists and revolutionaries throughout history have turned to it, again and again. From the suffragettes who smashed windows and chained themselves to fences, to the civil rights protesters who sat at whites-only lunch counters, to the environmentalists who scale skyscrapers to hang banners, propaganda of the deed is about creating moments that demand attention.

But it's not just about the drama. The best deeds are those that embody the values of the movement they represent. When Gandhi marched to the sea to make salt, defying British colonial laws, his act was both symbolic and practical. It was a way of saying, "We don't need you. We can take care of ourselves."

This is the challenge of propaganda of the deed: to create acts that are not only memorable but also meaningful. They need to resonate with people, to speak to their hopes and fears, to show them a glimpse of a better world—or the horrors of the one they already live in.

The Legacy of the Deed

So, what is propaganda of the deed? It's a philosophy, a tactic, a gamble. It's the belief that sometimes, you have to throw a stone into the pond to make the ripples spread.

But it's also more than that. It's a reminder that we have the power to act, even in the face of overwhelming odds. It's a call to arms for those who believe that the world can be changed, not just with words, but with courage, creativity, and conviction.

And maybe, just maybe, it's what we need now more than ever. Because people don't listen—not until you make them.

Chapter 2: Historical Context and Theoretical Roots

———

History, if you've paid any attention to it, is a river of blood. It flows thick and dark, fed by tributaries of war, rebellion, betrayal, and the occasional glimmer of hope. The late 19th century was no exception, a time when the river churned with industrial smoke and the screams of the poor, crushed beneath the relentless machinery of capitalism and monarchy.

It was in this boiling cauldron of suffering and injustice that the idea of *propaganda of the deed* was born. Like a spark struck from flint, it lit a fire in the hearts of those who believed that the world wasn't just unfair—it was unbearable—and that something had to be done about it. Not tomorrow, not after a committee meeting, but now, with action that would shatter the status quo.

To understand propaganda of the deed, we need to trace its roots. We need to go back to the philosophers and revolutionaries who dreamed it into existence, men who believed that words weren't enough to change the world. And let's be honest, words are a dime a dozen. Deeds, though? Deeds make history.

Mikhail Bakunin: The Revolutionary Firestarter

Let's start with Mikhail Bakunin. If there was ever a man who could embody the phrase "force of nature," it was him. Picture a bear of a man, bearded, wild-eyed, with a voice that could make walls tremble. Born in Russia in 1814, Bakunin grew up in a land where serfs toiled in misery while the nobility lived in gilded excess. He saw injustice everywhere, and instead of learning to accept it, he set out to destroy it.

Bakunin is best remembered as one of the fathers of anarchism, but don't let the label fool you. Anarchism, in his eyes, wasn't about chaos; it was about liberation. It was about tearing down systems of oppression and building a world where people could govern themselves, free from kings and capitalists alike.

But Bakunin didn't believe in waiting around for the perfect moment or the perfect conditions to act. That kind of thinking, he argued, was for cowards and bureaucrats. "The passion for destruction is a creative passion," he wrote, a phrase that would become a rallying cry for revolutionaries.

Bakunin believed that bold, dramatic action could inspire the masses. He wasn't naïve—he knew that one man with a stick of dynamite wasn't going to bring down an empire. But he believed that a single act of defiance, a single spark, could ignite a firestorm. And once that fire caught, it would spread, consuming the old world and giving birth to a new one.

Carlo Pisacane: Words Aren't Enough

If Bakunin was the hammer, Carlo Pisacane was the scalpel. An Italian revolutionary, Pisacane shared Bakunin's hatred of tyranny, but his approach was more calculated, more philosophical. Born in 1818, Pisacane grew up in a divided Italy, where foreign powers and local despots kept the people under their boot. He dreamed of a united, free Italy, and he was willing to die for that dream.

Pisacane believed in the power of action, but for him, it wasn't just about rebellion—it was about education. He argued that the masses wouldn't rise up on their own; they needed to be shown the way. And the best way to teach them, he said, was through example.

In his 1857 essay *Saggio sulla Rivoluzione*, Pisacane wrote:

"The propaganda of ideas is a chimera. Ideas result from deeds, not the other way around. The people will not be free when they are educated, but educated when they are free."

This was a radical notion. While many revolutionaries believed that education and enlightenment were the keys to liberation, Pisacane flipped the script. He argued that freedom itself was the best teacher. People wouldn't learn by reading pamphlets or attending lectures—they would learn by seeing revolutionaries in action, by witnessing their courage and sacrifice.

Pisacane didn't just talk the talk, either. In 1857, he led a doomed expedition to liberate southern Italy. With a small band of followers, he landed in the Kingdom of Naples, hoping to spark a peasant revolt. The uprising never materialized, and Pisacane was killed. But his death wasn't the end of his story. His martyrdom became a symbol of resistance, a seed that would grow into the Italian unification movement.

The Birth of Direct Action

By the late 19th century, the world was changing at a breakneck pace. Industrialization had transformed cities into sprawling, soot-covered nightmares, where factory owners grew fat while workers toiled in squalor. Empires expanded their reach, exploiting colonies and crushing resistance with ruthless efficiency. And yet, for all their power, these systems were fragile, like a pane of glass waiting for the right stone.

Revolutionary movements sprang up across Europe and beyond, fueled by a growing sense of injustice. Socialists, anarchists, and other radicals began to organize, but they faced a daunting challenge: how do you wake people up when they've been beaten down for so long?

This is where propaganda of the deed came in. It wasn't just a tactic; it was a philosophy, a way of cutting through the noise and forcing people to pay attention. The idea was simple: dramatic, symbolic actions could inspire the masses, shake the foundations of power, and show people that change was possible.

It wasn't about violence for its own sake—though violence was often part of the equation. It was about creating a moment that would stick in the public's mind, a moment that would make them question the world around them.

Anarchism and the Power of the Deed

Anarchism was fertile ground for the idea of propaganda of the deed. At its core, anarchism is about rejecting authority and embracing freedom, but it's also about direct action—taking matters into your own hands, rather than waiting for someone else to fix things.

For anarchists, propaganda of the deed was a way to bypass the endless debates and bureaucracy that plagued other political movements. Why waste time arguing when you could act? Why wait for permission when you could seize the moment?

The Seeds of Revolution

The late 19th century saw a wave of acts that embodied propaganda of the deed. These weren't random acts of violence; they were calculated, symbolic strikes against the systems of oppression.

One of the most infamous examples was the assassination of Tsar Alexander II in 1881. The Narodnaya Volya, a Russian revolutionary group, believed that killing the tsar would inspire the masses to rise up against the autocracy. They spent months planning the attack, evading the tsar's secret police, and smuggling explosives. When the bomb finally went off, killing the tsar, it sent shockwaves across the empire.

The assassination didn't bring down the Russian monarchy, but it sparked a wave of revolutionary activity and inspired radicals around the world. It was a bloody, desperate act, but it wasn't senseless. It was a message, written in fire and blood, that the old order was vulnerable.

The Theoretical Divide

Not everyone agreed on the merits of propaganda of the deed. Within the anarchist and socialist movements, there was fierce debate over whether dramatic acts were effective or counterproductive.

Some argued that such acts alienated the very people they were meant to inspire. After all, it's hard to win hearts and minds when your message comes wrapped in dynamite. Others pointed out that propaganda of the deed often led to brutal crackdowns, as governments used the acts as an excuse to crush dissent.

But for its proponents, the risks were worth it. They believed that bold action was the only way to cut through the noise and make people see the truth. They weren't interested in playing it safe—they were interested in making history.

A Philosophy of Courage

At its core, propaganda of the deed is about courage: the courage to act, to risk everything, to stand up against impossible odds. It's a philosophy born of desperation and hope, of anger and love.

It's easy to dismiss it as reckless or dangerous—and it is both of those things. But it's also a reminder that the world doesn't change on its own. It changes because people make it change, sometimes with words, sometimes with deeds, and sometimes with both.

The thinkers who dreamed up propaganda of the deed weren't perfect. They were flawed, messy, and often misguided. But they shared a belief that still resonates today: that when the world is broken, you can't just sit back and hope someone else will fix it.

Sometimes, you have to throw the first stone.

Chapter 3: The Philosophy of Action

There's a scene I think about sometimes, one of those grainy old clips you might stumble across in a documentary. Picture a quiet town square in 1930s Germany, just an ordinary day. The camera pans to a crowd of people raising their arms in the Nazi salute. They're all doing it, every last one of them—except for one man. He's standing there, arms crossed, jaw set, refusing to go along.

Now, I don't know that man's name. History doesn't either. He's just a blur in the crowd, a shadow against the tide. But when you see that clip, your eyes don't linger on the hundreds of raised arms; they're drawn to him, to the single point of defiance. In that moment, he's not just a man. He's a symbol.

That's the power of action. Words might explain his defiance. A manifesto might give it context. But none of that sticks in your mind like the sight of that one man refusing to salute. Deeds, you see, aren't just actions—they're stories, told in a language everyone understands.

Why Words Fail

Let's get one thing straight: words matter. A well-crafted speech can bring a crowd to its feet. A clever turn of phrase can stick in your head for days. But there's a reason politicians spend millions on advertising campaigns, why every revolution in history has needed more than just pamphlets and posters. Words alone aren't enough.

Why? Because words can be ignored.

We live in a world drowning in them, a constant barrage of slogans, headlines, tweets, and chatter. Your words are just one more drop in an ocean of noise. Even the best ideas, the ones that could actually change the world, can get lost in the din.

But deeds? Deeds are impossible to ignore. They cut through the noise like a scream in a quiet room.

Take the civil rights movement in America. Dr. Martin Luther King Jr. gave some of the greatest speeches in human history, words that still echo decades later. But it wasn't just his speeches that moved the needle—it was the images of Black men and women marching, sitting at segregated lunch counters, enduring police dogs and fire hoses.

Those deeds didn't just support the words—they amplified them. They made the injustice real, visible, undeniable.

The Language of Action

Here's the thing about deeds: they don't just say something; they *show* it. And what they show isn't just an idea—it's a commitment, a willingness to back up your beliefs with risk and effort.

Take the act of self-immolation. It's one of the most extreme forms of propaganda of the deed, and yet, when done, it leaves an indelible mark. Think of Thích Quảng Đức, the Buddhist monk who set himself on fire in 1963 to protest the persecution of Buddhists in South Vietnam. The image of his burning body, serene and unflinching, shocked the world.

Now, if Thích Quảng Đức had written a letter instead, would we still be talking about him? Would his protest have shaken governments and turned global attention to his cause? Unlikely. The deed spoke louder than any words ever could.

This is the philosophy of action in a nutshell: it's about understanding that sometimes, the only way to make people see is to make them feel.

The Urgency of Deeds

Here's a hard truth: most people don't act until they have to. They'll talk about change, nod along to speeches, maybe even sign a petition. But when push comes to shove, inertia takes over. Change is hard, after all, and people don't like hard things.

Deeds disrupt that inertia. They create urgency, a sense that the time for talk is over, that the moment to act is now.

Let's go back to the Montgomery bus boycott in 1955. It started with one woman—Rosa Parks—refusing to give up her seat on a segregated bus. Her act of defiance wasn't spontaneous; it was part of a broader strategy. But in that moment, it was just her, sitting there, saying, *No.*

That single act lit the fuse. It turned abstract ideas about civil rights into something real, something immediate. It said to people, "This is happening. This is your moment. What are you going to do about it?"

The philosophy of action isn't about waiting for the perfect time. It's about creating urgency, about forcing people to make a choice.

Deeds as Values

Deeds don't just communicate urgency—they embody values. When you take action, you're not just saying what you believe; you're living it.

Think of the Freedom Riders in the 1960s. These were men and women, Black and white, who rode buses through the segregated South to challenge Jim Crow laws. They knew they'd be beaten, arrested, maybe even killed. And they went anyway.

Their actions weren't just protests—they were a statement of values. They said, "We believe in equality so deeply that we're willing to risk everything for it." That kind of commitment is powerful. It makes people stop and think, "If they're willing to do this, maybe I should pay attention."

The same principle applies to acts of sabotage by environmental activists or hunger strikes by political prisoners. These deeds aren't just about disrupting the system—they're about showing the world what you stand for, in the clearest, most undeniable terms.

The Risk of Action

Let's not sugarcoat it: deeds are dangerous. They can backfire, provoke backlash, or paint you as a villain instead of a hero.

Take the Haymarket affair in 1886. What started as a peaceful rally for workers' rights turned into chaos when someone threw a bomb into the crowd, killing police officers and protesters alike. The incident led to a brutal crackdown on the labor movement and the execution of several anarchists.

But here's the thing: risk is part of the equation. The very fact that deeds are risky is what makes them powerful. They show that you're willing to put something on the line—your safety, your freedom, even your life. And that willingness to risk speaks volumes.

This doesn't mean that every act of defiance is wise or effective. It means that deeds, by their nature, are a gamble. But when they pay off, they can change the course of history.

Igniting Movements

The ultimate goal of propaganda of the deed isn't just to make a statement—it's to ignite a movement. One act, no matter how bold, won't change the world on its own. But it can inspire others to act, creating a ripple effect that spreads far beyond the original deed.

Think of the Stonewall riots in 1969. They began as a spontaneous act of defiance against police harassment, led by LGBTQ+ people who had endured years of persecution. But that single night of resistance became the spark for a global movement.

The philosophy of action recognizes that change is never just about one person or one act. It's about lighting a fire in others, showing them what's possible, and giving them the courage to stand up and act.

A Call to Arms

The philosophy of action isn't for the faint of heart. It's about stepping into the arena, knowing you might lose. It's about risking failure, ridicule, and even harm to make a statement that can't be ignored.

But here's the thing: every great movement in history has needed people willing to take that risk. It's needed people who understand that words alone won't cut it, that sometimes you have to act, even if you're scared, even if you're not sure it'll work.

Because in the end, deeds are what make history. Deeds are what remind us that change is possible, even in the face of overwhelming odds.

So if you're sitting there, wondering what you can do, here's the answer: act.

The world doesn't change on its own. Someone has to light the match. Will it be you?

Chapter 4: The Spectrum of Deeds

The first thing you need to understand about propaganda of the deed is that it's not a one-size-fits-all affair. It's not a hammer you take to every problem, smashing away until something cracks. No, it's more like a toolbox—different tools for different jobs. And just like tools, some are blunt, some are sharp, and some are downright dangerous if you don't know what you're doing.

But here's the rub: no matter the method, every deed carries the same goal—to provoke, to inspire, to send a message so loud and clear that even the deaf and willfully ignorant have no choice but to pay attention.

So, what kind of tools are we talking about? To answer that, we need to unpack the spectrum of deeds, from the fiery violence of insurrection to the quiet, stubborn bravery of civil disobedience. Each has its place, and each comes with its own risks and rewards.

At the Edge of Fire: Violent Insurrection

Let's start at the sharp end of the spectrum. When people think of propaganda of the deed, their minds often go here first: the bomb throwers, the gunmen, the shadowy figures plotting in darkened rooms. And why not? Violence grabs headlines. It's the loudest tool in the box, the one that guarantees people will sit up and take notice.

The late 19th century, the cradle of propaganda of the deed, was full of such acts. Anarchists assassinated kings and presidents. They bombed stock exchanges and police stations. These weren't random outbursts—they were calculated strikes against symbols of power, designed to shake the pillars of society.

Take, for instance, the assassination of President William McKinley in 1901. Leon Czolgosz, a self-proclaimed anarchist, shot McKinley during a public reception. Czolgosz later said he acted because he believed it was his duty to strike a blow against tyranny and inequality.

The impact was immediate and profound. McKinley's death led to a massive crackdown on anarchists and leftist movements across the United States. But it also forced the nation to confront the deep divisions between the rich and the poor, between the powerful and the powerless.

That's the double-edged nature of violent deeds. They grab attention, sure, but they can also alienate the very people you're trying to inspire. For every person who sees an assassin as a hero, there's another who sees them as a monster.

Violence is a hammer, and sometimes a hammer is what you need. But it's a blunt instrument, and you'd better be damn sure what you're swinging it at.

The Power of Sabotage

Not every violent deed involves taking lives. Sometimes, the goal isn't to kill but to disrupt, to throw a wrench into the gears of the machine. That's where sabotage comes in.

Think of the Luddites in 19th-century England, smashing textile machines to protest the industrialization that was stealing their livelihoods. Or the French Resistance during World War II, sabotaging Nazi rail lines and communication networks.

Sabotage walks a fine line. It's destructive, yes, but it often carries a moral clarity that outright violence lacks. Breaking a machine is one thing; killing a man is another.

In the 1970s, environmental activists began using sabotage as a form of propaganda of the deed. Groups like Earth First! and the Sea Shepherd Conservation Society disrupted logging operations, whaling ships, and other industries they saw as threats to the planet. Their actions were dramatic, often illegal, and always designed to draw attention to their cause.

And it worked. The media covered their exploits, people started talking about deforestation and overfishing, and governments were forced to respond. Sabotage didn't solve the problems overnight, but it made people pay attention—and sometimes, that's the first step.

The Middle Ground: Direct Confrontation

Somewhere between violence and nonviolence lies the territory of direct confrontation. These are the actions that challenge authority head-on, often at great personal risk.

Take the sit-ins of the civil rights movement. Black students would walk into segregated lunch counters, sit down, and refuse to leave. They didn't shout or throw punches—they just sat there, knowing full well they'd be arrested, beaten, or worse.

These acts weren't violent, but they weren't passive, either. They were a direct challenge to an unjust system, a way of saying, "We're not moving until you deal with us."

The beauty of direct confrontation is its simplicity. You don't need bombs or elaborate plans—just courage and a willingness to stand your ground.

But make no mistake: this kind of action is still dangerous. The risk isn't just physical; it's psychological. Standing up to power, especially when you're alone or in a small group, takes a toll. But when done right, it can be incredibly effective.

Civil Disobedience: The Quiet Revolution

At the far end of the spectrum lies civil disobedience. This is the tool of Gandhi, of Thoreau, of millions of ordinary people who've decided that sometimes, the best way to fight the system is to refuse to play by its rules.

Civil disobedience is about breaking laws, but not just any laws—unjust ones. It's about saying, "This system doesn't represent me, so I'm not going to follow its rules."

The Montgomery bus boycott is a perfect example. For over a year, Black residents of Montgomery, Alabama, refused to ride the city's buses, protesting segregation. Their boycott crippled the transit system, forcing the city to change its policies.

Civil disobedience works because it's hard to demonize. It's peaceful, it's principled, and it puts the onus on the oppressors to react. When the state responds with violence or repression, it only proves the protesters' point.

But here's the catch: civil disobedience requires patience. It's a slow burn, not a flash of lightning. You don't see immediate results, and that can be frustrating. But when it works, it can reshape society in ways that violent insurrection never could.

The Gray Areas

Of course, not every act fits neatly into a category. Some blur the lines between violence and nonviolence, between confrontation and civil disobedience.

Take the Zapatista uprising in 1994. The Zapatistas, a group of Indigenous rebels in Mexico, declared war on the government, occupying towns and engaging in armed clashes with the military. But they didn't just rely on violence. They used the media to spread their message, holding press conferences and issuing communiqués.

Their goal wasn't just to fight—it was to tell a story, to show the world what was happening to Indigenous people in Mexico. And it worked. The Zapatistas became a global symbol of resistance, inspiring activists around the world.

This kind of hybrid action is risky. It's harder to control the narrative, harder to predict how people will react. But when it works, it can be incredibly powerful.

Choosing Your Tool

So, how do you decide which tool to use? That's the million-dollar question, isn't it?

The answer depends on your goals, your audience, and your willingness to take risks. Violent deeds grab attention but can alienate people. Nonviolent deeds take longer but build broader support. And the gray areas? They're a gamble, one that requires careful planning and a bit of luck.

The key is to understand that no deed exists in a vacuum. Every action sends a message, and that message will be interpreted in ways you can't always control.

But here's the thing: doing nothing isn't an option. The world is full of people who benefit from the status quo, people who'll do everything in their power to keep things just the way they are. The only way to change that is to act.

The Cost of Inaction

There's a story I heard once, about a town where a dam was about to break. The townsfolk knew the danger—they could see the cracks, hear the water roaring on the other side. But no one did anything. They waited, hoping someone else would fix it, until the dam finally burst and swept them all away.

That's the cost of inaction.

Propaganda of the deed is about refusing to be swept away. It's about saying, "I see the cracks, and I'm not going to wait for someone else to fix them."

Whether you pick up a hammer or a protest sign, whether you act alone or with a crowd, the important thing is that you act. Because the alternative—the silence, the waiting—is a slow death, for you and for the world.

So, what's it going to be? Are you ready to choose your tool? Because the dam's not going to hold much longer.

Chapter 5: Ethics of the Deed

The room was dim, lit only by a single bulb dangling from the ceiling like a tired old man hanging by his necktie. The table beneath it was scratched and scarred, its wood gouged with deep lines like the wrinkles of a face that had seen too much. On that table, between two strangers, sat a revolver.

One of the strangers spoke first. "You sure about this?"

The other man's face was pale but determined. "I am."

The first man nodded. He reached for the gun, spun the cylinder, and snapped it shut with a harsh metallic click. "All right," he said. "Let's see what kind of man you really are."

This isn't the kind of scene you'd find in a philosophy textbook, but it might as well be. Because the ethics of propaganda of the deed often boil down to one question: *How far are you willing to go?*

The Cost of Conviction

You've probably heard the saying, "The road to hell is paved with good intentions." It's a tidy little phrase, but it doesn't do justice to the messy business of real-world ethics. In real life, the road isn't paved at all—it's muddy, full of potholes, and so shrouded in fog that you can't tell if you're heading toward paradise or the edge of a cliff.

Propaganda of the deed lives in that fog. It's about action, about taking a stand, about saying, *This is wrong, and I won't stand for it any longer.* But with action comes consequence, and with consequence comes moral responsibility.

Let's say you blow up a government building to protest corruption. You plan it carefully, making sure it's empty at the time. But the janitor, who works late on Tuesdays, doesn't get the memo. He dies in the explosion.

Now what? Was your act justified because it targeted a corrupt system? Or does the janitor's death taint everything you were trying to achieve?

That's the ethical minefield of propaganda of the deed. Every action has ripples, and those ripples can carry you to places you never intended to go.

The Violence Dilemma

Let's talk about the elephant in the room: violence. It's the part of propaganda of the deed that makes people uncomfortable, the thing that separates it from more "respectable" forms of protest.

But violence isn't a monolith. It's a spectrum, ranging from the targeted assassination of a dictator to the smashing of a store window during a riot. And every act of violence comes with its own set of ethical questions.

Here's a scenario for you: You're living under a brutal dictatorship. People are being tortured, killed, disappeared. You decide to take matters into your own hands and assassinate the dictator. You succeed, but in the chaos that follows, a power vacuum opens up, and things get even worse.

Does that mean your act was wrong? Or does the responsibility lie with the people who failed to build a better system in the aftermath?

Now flip the script. Let's say you choose not to act. The dictator stays in power, and the killings continue. Does your inaction make you complicit?

That's the thing about violence—it's never just about the act itself. It's about what comes before and after, about the context and the consequences. And the ethical lines are rarely as clear as we'd like them to be.

Collateral Damage

One of the thorniest issues in propaganda of the deed is collateral damage. This isn't just about unintended deaths or injuries—it's about the wider impact of your actions on the very people you're trying to help.

Let's go back to the Haymarket affair of 1886. A bomb thrown during a labor rally killed several police officers and civilians. The event sparked a massive crackdown on labor unions and anarchist groups, setting the workers' movement back years.

The question is: was the bomb justified? The person who threw it might have believed they were striking a blow against oppression, but the end result was more oppression, not less.

Collateral damage isn't always physical, either. Sometimes it's about perception. A violent act that's intended to inspire resistance can just as easily inspire fear or apathy. It can give your enemies the ammunition they need to paint you as a villain, undermining your cause in the process.

That's why the ethics of the deed require not just conviction, but foresight. It's not enough to ask, *What do I want to achieve?* You also have to ask, *What might I destroy in the process?*

The Justification Question

Every act of propaganda of the deed starts with a justification. It's the thing that lets you look in the mirror and say, "This is right. This is necessary." But justification is a slippery beast, and it's all too easy to justify things in hindsight.

Think of the French Revolution. The storming of the Bastille, the executions, the Reign of Terror—all of it was justified in the name of liberty, equality, and fraternity. But at what point did those justifications cross the line?

History is full of similar examples. The suffragettes who bombed buildings and slashed paintings in their fight for women's rights. The Weather Underground, who bombed government buildings to protest the Vietnam War. The eco-terrorists who spike trees to stop logging operations, knowing it could maim the workers who try to cut them down.

In every case, the people involved believed they were acting for the greater good. But belief isn't the same as truth, and the line between righteous defiance and reckless destruction is thinner than you think.

So how do you know if your deed is justified? How do you weigh the potential good against the potential harm?

The Question of Consent

One of the most troubling aspects of propaganda of the deed is that it often involves making decisions for other people—decisions they might not agree with.

Let's say you're an environmental activist. You blow up a dam to save a river, but the people living downstream relied on that dam for electricity. They didn't ask you to act on their behalf, but now they're living in darkness because of your decision.

This is the ethical tightrope that every revolutionary walks. On one hand, you're fighting for a cause you believe in. On the other hand, your actions have consequences for people who might not share your beliefs.

Does the end justify the means? Or does the lack of consent invalidate your cause, no matter how noble it might be?

Moral Absolutism vs. Moral Relativism

At its core, the ethics of the deed are a clash between two worldviews: moral absolutism and moral relativism.

The absolutists say, "There are lines you don't cross, no matter what." They believe in universal principles—don't kill, don't harm, don't lie—and see any violation of those principles as a failure.

The relativists, on the other hand, say, "Context is everything." They believe that ethics are situational, that what's right or wrong depends on the circumstances.

Propaganda of the deed often forces you to pick a side. Are you willing to break an absolute rule—like the prohibition against violence—for the sake of a greater good? Or do you believe that some rules are sacred, even if it means sacrificing your goals?

Living with the Consequences

Here's the thing about ethics: they don't stop mattering once the deed is done. In fact, that's when they matter most.

Imagine you've taken a drastic action—let's say you've assassinated a corrupt official. The media is in a frenzy, the government is cracking down, and you're sitting in a safe house, waiting for the fallout.

What happens next? Do you feel justified, even proud? Or do the doubts start to creep in?

History is full of revolutionaries who were haunted by their deeds, who spent the rest of their lives wondering if they'd done the right thing. Because propaganda of the deed isn't just about changing the world—it's about living with the choices you've made.

The Courage to Question

If there's one thing I've learned, it's that the people who do the most damage are the ones who never question themselves. The ones who act with absolute certainty, who believe they're on the right side of history and refuse to consider the possibility that they might be wrong.

The ethics of the deed aren't about finding easy answers. They're about asking hard questions, about wrestling with doubt, about being willing to change course if the path you're on starts to feel wrong.

Because in the end, ethics aren't just about what you do—they're about who you become.

So before you pick up that hammer, that torch, that gun, ask yourself this: *Am I ready to live with the consequences? Am I ready to look myself in the eye and say, "This was worth it"?*

If the answer is yes, then go ahead. Take your stand. Do your deed.

But if the answer is no? Then maybe it's time to set the gun down and walk away.

Chapter 6: The Assassination of Alexander II (1881)

The morning of March 13, 1881, was deceptively serene. Snow blanketed the cobbled streets of St. Petersburg, muffling the sounds of the city like a great cotton quilt. Horse-drawn carriages trundled along the avenues, their wheels crunching softly through the icy slush. Inside one of those carriages, seated beneath the royal crest, was a man who had been called many things: the Tsar Liberator, the White Czar, the Great Reformer.

But to the people who had spent months planning his death, Alexander II was nothing more than an obstacle—a symbol of an autocratic regime that had to be destroyed if Russia was ever to be free.

That morning, the Narodnaya Volya—"The People's Will"—intended to ensure that Alexander's name would go down in history for one reason and one reason only: he was the first Russian emperor to die by assassination.

The Reformer and the Regime

To understand why Alexander II was targeted, you first need to understand the paradox of the man himself. On one hand, he was a reformer. This was the Tsar who, in 1861, had abolished serfdom, freeing millions of peasants from a feudal system that had kept them in bondage for centuries.

But for all his reforms, Alexander was still an autocrat. His rule wasn't guided by a constitution or a parliament but by the ironclad authority of the Romanov dynasty. While he offered freedom with one hand, he clenched the other in a fist, ready to crush dissent.

By the 1870s, dissatisfaction with the regime was boiling over. The intelligentsia, students, and radicals had grown impatient with the slow pace of reform. They demanded more—land for the peasants, political freedom, and an end to the oppressive machinery of the state.

Out of this cauldron of discontent emerged Narodnaya Volya, a revolutionary organization dedicated to one idea: that dramatic, decisive acts of violence could ignite a spark that would burn through the autocracy.

The idea was simple, brutal, and rooted in the philosophy of propaganda of the deed. If they could assassinate Alexander II—the living embodiment of the Russian state—it would send a message that no ruler was invincible. More than that, it would inspire the masses to rise up and claim the freedom they deserved.

Or so they hoped.

THE PLAN

Killing a tsar was no small feat. Alexander II rarely appeared in public without a heavy guard, and his movements were unpredictable, designed to thwart potential attackers. But Narodnaya Volya was nothing if not determined.

For months, they planned and plotted, refining their methods and studying Alexander's routine. They dug a tunnel under one of the streets he was known to travel, filling it with explosives. When that failed, they regrouped and devised a new plan—one that would rely on the element of surprise and the bravery of their members.

The leader of the operation was Andrei Zhelyabov, a revolutionary with a quiet intensity that masked his ruthless determination. Under his command were several key players, including Sophia Perovskaya, a woman whose steely resolve and tactical brilliance would become the stuff of legend.

Their plan was both simple and audacious: they would intercept Alexander's carriage on one of his Sunday outings and use hand-thrown bombs to kill him. Each bomb was packed with dynamite and shrapnel, designed to cause maximum destruction.

There was no room for error, and no expectation of survival.

The Ambush

On the morning of March 13, Perovskaya stood at the edge of Catherine Canal, her face pale but calm against the cold. She signaled to the others with a white handkerchief as Alexander's carriage approached. The scene was almost pastoral—snow falling gently, the canal frozen solid beneath a thin crust of ice.

But beneath the surface, tension crackled like static electricity.

The first bomb was thrown by Nikolai Rysakov, a young recruit eager to prove his commitment to the cause. It struck the ground near the carriage, exploding in a deafening roar. The shockwave shattered windows, sprayed the street with debris, and injured several of the guards riding behind the tsar.

When the smoke cleared, Alexander's carriage lay in splinters. But the tsar himself had survived, shielded by the heavy armor of the vehicle. Dazed but unharmed, he stepped out of the wreckage to assess the damage.

That moment—the tsar standing exposed in the open—was the opportunity the revolutionaries had been waiting for.

As Alexander moved toward Rysakov, who had been captured by the guards, another conspirator stepped forward. Ignacy Hryniewiecki, a pale, wiry man with sunken eyes, clutched the second bomb in his hands. He threw it directly at the tsar's feet.

The Blast

The second explosion was devastating. Shrapnel tore through the air, cutting down everyone within range. Alexander II, once the most powerful man in Russia, crumpled to the ground in a pool of his own blood. His legs were mangled, his abdomen torn open, his face pale and shock-stricken.

Hryniewiecki didn't live to see the aftermath. The bomb had killed him instantly, along with several bystanders. The street was a scene of utter carnage, a macabre tableau of blood, snow, and twisted bodies.

As his guards rushed to his side, Alexander managed to whisper a few words: "Take me to the palace... to die there."

But he never made it. Within hours, the Tsar Liberator was dead.

The Aftermath

The assassination of Alexander II sent shockwaves through Russia and the world. For Narodnaya Volya, it was the culmination of years of effort, a strike at the heart of the autocracy. But the result wasn't the revolution they had hoped for.

Instead of inspiring the masses to rise up, the assassination provoked a brutal crackdown. The new tsar, Alexander III, was a reactionary who saw his father's death as proof that reform was futile. He rolled back many of the changes Alexander II had implemented and unleashed a wave of repression that decimated the revolutionary movement.

Narodnaya Volya itself was destroyed within a year. Most of its members, including Zhelyabov and Perovskaya, were arrested, tried, and executed. Their dream of a free and just Russia was buried alongside them.

A Legacy Written in Blood

The assassination of Alexander II remains one of the most infamous examples of propaganda of the deed—a dramatic, violent act designed to send a message and inspire action.

But what message did it send?

PROPAGANDA OF THE DEED

To some, it was a heroic act of defiance, proof that even the most powerful tyrants could be brought low. To others, it was a senseless act of terror that achieved nothing but more suffering.

The truth, as always, lies somewhere in between.

For the revolutionaries of Narodnaya Volya, the assassination was a statement of principles—a refusal to accept the status quo, even at the cost of their own lives. But it also highlighted the dangers of relying on violence as a catalyst for change.

Violence, after all, is unpredictable. It can inspire, but it can also alienate. It can break the chains of oppression, but it can just as easily tighten them.

The death of Alexander II didn't bring about the revolution Narodnaya Volya had dreamed of. But it did something else: it forced the world to confront the contradictions of power and reform, of oppression and resistance.

And maybe that's the real legacy of propaganda of the deed—not the act itself, but the questions it leaves behind. Questions that, even now, have no easy answers.

So here's one to ponder: if you were standing on that snowy street in St. Petersburg, bomb in hand, knowing everything that came after—would you still throw it?

Chapter 7: The Haymarket Affair (1886)

Some events come like thunderclaps, splitting the sky open and shaking the ground beneath your feet. The Haymarket Affair was one of those events—a flash of lightning that illuminated everything wrong with the world before plunging it into even deeper shadows.

The date was May 4, 1886, but the story didn't begin there. No, it started long before the bomb was thrown, long before the gallows creaked under the weight of the accused. It began in the factories, in the foundries, in the sweat-soaked rooms where men and women worked their lives away for pennies, their hands raw and their spirits bent.

It began with a demand so simple it sounded almost laughable to the industrial barons of the day: an eight-hour workday.

The Struggle for Eight Hours

By the late 19th century, the United States was a machine, and its fuel was human misery. Workers toiled from sunrise to well past sunset, sometimes 12 or 16 hours a day, six days a week, in conditions that would make your stomach churn. Children lost fingers to whirring blades, lungs filled with coal dust, and bodies broke down before their time.

But in 1884, the Federation of Organized Trades and Labor Unions declared that enough was enough. They set May 1, 1886, as the deadline for the eight-hour workday to become the law of the land. If it didn't, they warned, the workers would strike.

May 1 came and went, and the law didn't budge. So the workers did what they'd promised: they walked out. Across the country, hundreds of thousands of men and women left their jobs, demanding better conditions, better pay, and, most of all, an eight-hour day.

Chicago was the epicenter of the movement. It was a city of smoke and steel, where the working class was large, angry, and organized. Labor leaders, socialists, and anarchists had been agitating there for years, stirring up discontent and calling for radical change.

And on May 3, the tension that had been simmering finally boiled over.

The McCormick Riot

That day, striking workers gathered outside the McCormick Reaper Works, a factory on Chicago's South Side. They were met by scabs—replacement workers brought in to break the strike—and by the police, who were there to protect the scabs.

When the striking workers tried to confront the scabs, the police opened fire. Four workers were killed, and dozens more were injured.

For the anarchists of Chicago, the massacre at McCormick was the final straw. They called for a mass protest the following evening at Haymarket Square, a bustling marketplace in the heart of the city. The purpose, they said, was to denounce police brutality and demand justice for the slain workers.

What they got instead was chaos.

The Haymarket Bombing

May 4 was an unseasonably cool evening, and the turnout at Haymarket Square was smaller than expected. A few thousand people gathered to hear speeches by labor leaders and anarchists, but as the night wore on, the crowd began to thin. By the time the last speaker, Samuel Fielden, took the stage, only a few hundred people remained.

The police, however, weren't taking any chances. As Fielden spoke, a line of officers marched toward the square, their boots echoing against the cobblestones.

And then it happened.

No one knows exactly who threw the bomb. Maybe it was one of the anarchists, enraged by the McCormick killings. Maybe it was an agent provocateur, sent to discredit the labor movement. Maybe it was a lone wolf, acting on their own twisted sense of justice.

But whoever it was, the bomb—a crudely made device packed with dynamite and shrapnel—exploded with devastating force.

PROPAGANDA OF THE DEED

The blast killed one officer instantly and injured dozens more, some of whom would die later from their wounds. The police, panicked and enraged, opened fire on the crowd. In the chaos that followed, civilians and officers alike were shot, trampled, and beaten.

By the time the smoke cleared, Haymarket Square was a scene of carnage.

The Aftermath

The bombing sent shockwaves through Chicago, through the labor movement, and through the nation. The newspapers had a field day, painting the anarchists as bloodthirsty radicals hellbent on destroying civilization. The authorities, eager to crush the labor movement, launched a sweeping crackdown.

They rounded up dozens of anarchists, socialists, and labor leaders, some of whom had been nowhere near Haymarket Square that night. Eight men were eventually put on trial, accused of conspiring to commit murder.

The trial was a travesty. The prosecution had no concrete evidence linking the defendants to the bombing, but that didn't matter. The real crime, as far as the court was concerned, was their political beliefs.

The judge openly declared that anarchism was on trial, not just the men in the dock. Witnesses were bribed or coerced, and the jury was stacked with men who openly admitted their bias against the defendants.

In the end, seven of the eight were sentenced to death.

The Martyrs

The convicted men became known as the Haymarket Martyrs, and their names—August Spies, Albert Parsons, Adolph Fischer, George Engel, and the others—became rallying cries for the labor movement.

On November 11, 1887, four of them were hanged. Louis Lingg, the youngest of the group, cheated the gallows by biting down on a smuggled dynamite cap in his cell, blowing his head apart in an act of defiance.

The other three were eventually pardoned, but by then, the damage was done. The executions had cemented the Haymarket Affair as one of the darkest moments in American labor history.

A Symbolic Victory

Here's the thing about Haymarket: in the short term, it was a disaster. The labor movement was vilified, the anarchist movement was decimated, and the fight for the eight-hour day stalled.

But in the long term? It became something else entirely.

The Haymarket Martyrs were celebrated as heroes, not just in the United States but around the world. Their sacrifice gave the labor movement a powerful symbol of resistance and solidarity. In 1889, the International Socialist Conference declared May 1—May Day—a global day of labor solidarity in their honor.

Haymarket didn't kill the labor movement. It made it stronger.

PROPAGANDA OF THE DEED

The Meaning of the Deed

The bombing at Haymarket Square was a classic example of propaganda of the deed—a dramatic, symbolic act meant to inspire and provoke. But it also illustrated the dangers of such acts.

Did the bomb thrower achieve their goal? It's hard to say. They brought attention to the brutality of the police and the desperation of the workers, but they also gave the state an excuse to crack down hard on the movement.

That's the paradox of propaganda of the deed: it can inspire, but it can also backfire.

Haymarket wasn't just a battle over workers' rights—it was a battle over meaning. To the authorities, it was proof of the dangers of radicalism. To the workers, it was a reminder of the price of resistance.

And for us, looking back, it's a story that raises uncomfortable questions.

When is violence justified? When does resistance become terror? And how do you fight a system that holds all the power without becoming just like it?

The answers aren't easy. But then, they never are.

The Legacy

Today, Haymarket Square is just another corner of Chicago, its cobblestones replaced by asphalt, its market stalls long gone.

But the echoes of that night in 1886 are still there, if you know where to listen.

The workers who died for the eight-hour day didn't live to see it become the norm, but their struggle paved the way for the rights we take for granted now.

And the Haymarket Martyrs? They didn't just die for labor rights. They died for the idea that ordinary people have the power to stand up to injustice, even when the odds are stacked against them.

So the next time you clock out after eight hours, remember this: someone, somewhere, threw a bomb so you wouldn't have to work twelve.

Chapter 8: Suffragette Militancy

There's something about a window smashing that grabs your attention. The clean, orderly world you think you know—your neat little shopfronts, your unbroken panes of glass—suddenly has a jagged edge. You hear the shatter before you see it, the sharp crack of something small and solid connecting with something fragile and defenseless.

In the early 20th century, women across England and beyond picked up rocks, hammers, and even hatchets, and went to work on those windows. Not because they were vandals. Not because they were criminals or bored or unhinged.

They smashed because no one would listen.

The suffragettes had tried everything else: polite petitions, reasoned debate, peaceful marches, even begging for justice. And still, the men in power turned their backs, dismissing them with a wave of the hand or a sneering, paternal smile.

So they smashed.

And when the windows broke, when the public gasped, when the papers screamed *"militants"* and *"lunatics,"* people finally started paying attention.

From Suffragists to Suffragettes

The story of suffragette militancy doesn't begin with broken glass or scorched buildings. It begins with frustration, with years—no, decades—of being ignored.

The women's suffrage movement in Britain formally took root in the mid-19th century. For years, it was led by women like Millicent Fawcett, who championed peaceful, law-abiding activism through the National Union of Women's Suffrage Societies (NUWSS). These were the suffragists—dedicated, patient, and committed to winning the vote by convincing men in Parliament to grant it to them.

But by the early 20th century, patience was running out. The world was changing. Industrialization had pulled women out of the domestic sphere and into factories, offices, and schools. They were working, organizing, and educating themselves. But politically, they were still powerless.

The frustration boiled over in 1903 when Emmeline Pankhurst founded the Women's Social and Political Union (WSPU). The WSPU wasn't about tea parties and polite pamphlets. Its motto was direct and uncompromising: *"Deeds, not words."*

That motto would come to define the suffragette movement and cement its place in the history of propaganda of the deed.

The Escalation Begins

At first, the suffragettes' actions were tame enough to avoid scandal. They heckled politicians during speeches, stormed into meetings, and chained themselves to railings outside government buildings. These stunts were meant to disrupt the daily flow of power, to make it impossible for the men in charge to ignore the cries for women's suffrage.

And for a while, it worked. The press took notice, albeit with a tone of mocking disdain. The authorities were annoyed but not alarmed. The suffragettes were a nuisance, but they weren't yet a threat.

That changed in 1908 when suffragettes Mary Leigh and Edith New smashed the windows of 10 Downing Street with stones wrapped in paper bearing the words *"Votes for Women."* It was a bold act, unprecedented in its sheer defiance. The papers roared, the public clutched their pearls, and the government, for the first time, responded with more than just indifference.

Leigh and New were arrested, tried, and sentenced to prison. They went willingly, proudly even, turning their imprisonment into another act of protest.

This marked a turning point. The suffragettes had discovered something powerful: breaking the law got results.

Fire, Glass, and Ink

By 1912, the suffragette campaign had grown more militant and more audacious. Under the leadership of Emmeline Pankhurst and her daughters Christabel and Sylvia, the WSPU declared an all-out war on property.

They smashed windows in London's busiest shopping districts, targeting high-profile establishments like Harrods and Fortnum & Mason. They slashed paintings in museums, including the famous Rokeby Venus at the National Gallery.

They set fire to postboxes, destroying letters and parcels in a symbolic attack on the government's communication system.

Some suffragettes escalated further, planting crude bombs in empty buildings and pouring acid into golf course holes—acts that walked the fine line between sabotage and terrorism.

Each act of destruction came with a message, scrawled on a piece of paper or etched into the public consciousness by the headlines: *"This is what happens when you deny justice."*

The Hunger Strikes

For all their militancy, the suffragettes' most powerful weapon wasn't a rock or a match. It was their own bodies.

When suffragettes were arrested—and they were arrested often—they used their imprisonment as a stage for further protest. They demanded to be treated as political prisoners, not common criminals, and when that demand was ignored, they turned to hunger strikes.

The hunger strikes were brutal, both for the women who undertook them and for the authorities who tried to suppress them. Prison officials, horrified at the prospect of suffragettes starving to death on their watch, resorted to force-feeding—a gruesome process that involved restraining the women, forcing a tube down their throats, and pouring liquid food directly into their stomachs.

The procedure was as painful as it was humiliating, and it often left the women with permanent injuries. But the suffragettes endured it, knowing that every forced feeding was another headline, another piece of evidence for their cause.

The public was horrified, not by the suffragettes' militancy but by the government's response. Suddenly, the women who had been painted as dangerous extremists looked more like martyrs, and the suffrage movement gained a wave of sympathy.

Emmeline Pankhurst: The Relentless Leader

At the center of it all was Emmeline Pankhurst, a woman who embodied the suffragette spirit. She was charismatic, fierce, and utterly uncompromising.

Pankhurst believed that militancy wasn't just justified—it was necessary. She argued that women had been excluded from the political process for so long that polite methods were no longer enough. If men were moved to action by broken glass and burning buildings, then so be it.

"We are here not because we are law-breakers; we are here in our efforts to become law-makers," Pankhurst declared in one of her most famous speeches.

Her leadership made her a hero to some and a villain to others, but no one could ignore her.

Backlash and Victory

Of course, the suffragettes' militancy came with a price. Their actions alienated some members of the public, including other women who felt that the WSPU's tactics were too extreme. Even within the suffrage movement, there was dissent.

The government, meanwhile, responded with increasing brutality. Suffragettes were beaten, arrested, and vilified in the press. The Cat and Mouse Act of 1913 allowed the authorities to release hunger-striking suffragettes from prison, only to re-arrest them once they had recovered.

But for all the backlash, the suffragettes succeeded in one crucial way: they forced the issue of women's suffrage into the national spotlight.

When World War I broke out in 1914, the suffragettes paused their militant campaign to support the war effort. Their contributions, along with the decades of agitation that preceded them, helped shift public opinion.

In 1918, women over 30 gained the right to vote in Britain, and by 1928, the vote was extended to all women over 21.

The Legacy of Militancy

The suffragette movement is a study in the power of propaganda of the deed. Their acts of militancy were calculated, symbolic, and unapologetically disruptive.

They smashed windows not because they enjoyed destruction but because they understood its power to make people pay attention. They endured hunger strikes not because they wanted to suffer but because their suffering exposed the cruelty of the system.

And in the end, their deeds worked.

But their story also raises questions—about the ethics of militancy, about the line between protest and terrorism, about the price of justice.

Would women have won the vote without the suffragettes? Perhaps. But it's hard to imagine that victory coming as swiftly or as decisively without their militancy.

And so we remember them—the women who threw stones and lit fires, who starved themselves and suffered for a cause they believed was worth any price.

Because sometimes, when no one will listen, you have to break a few windows.

Chapter 9: The Black Panthers and the Power of Presence

The Black Panthers didn't just walk into a room. They stormed in, armed with shotguns, wearing leather jackets and berets, carrying themselves with the kind of defiance that told you they weren't asking for respect—they were taking it.

This wasn't politeness. This wasn't the sanitized, well-behaved activism the mainstream liked to celebrate. The Panthers were there to disrupt, to challenge, to push back. Every time they appeared—at a rally, a courthouse, or patrolling the streets—they sent a message that was impossible to ignore: *we will defend ourselves, and we will take care of our people if you won't.*

If propaganda of the deed is about action as message, then the Black Panther Party perfected it. They didn't just talk about oppression; they confronted it. They didn't just demand justice; they created it. And they didn't just critique the system—they made sure the system knew they weren't afraid to fight back.

A Nation on Fire

To understand the Black Panthers, you have to understand the firestorm they were born into. The late 1960s in America was a time of upheaval, rage, and bloodshed. Cities burned as Black communities, long simmering under the weight of systemic racism and police brutality, erupted in rebellion.

Martin Luther King Jr. had been assassinated, his dream of peaceful resistance seeming increasingly out of reach. Malcolm X, who had preached Black self-defense, had also been gunned down. The Vietnam War raged on, with Black men drafted and sent to die in disproportionate numbers for a country that treated them as second-class citizens.

And then there were the police.

The 1960s were a golden age for white supremacy in blue uniforms. In Black neighborhoods, police weren't just enforcers of the law—they were occupiers. They beat, harassed, and humiliated with impunity. People knew their names not because they protected but because they terrorized.

It was in this crucible of anger and despair that the Black Panther Party for Self-Defense was born.

The Birth of the Panthers

In October 1966, in Oakland, California, two men—Huey P. Newton and Bobby Seale—sat down and wrote out a 10-point platform. It was a manifesto, a declaration of what the Panthers stood for: decent housing, fair employment, an end to police brutality, and, most importantly, self-determination for Black people.

But the Panthers weren't just about words. Words were fine, sure. Inspiring even. But Newton and Seale understood something that set them apart: words without action are just noise.

So they armed themselves—not metaphorically, but literally. California law at the time allowed citizens to carry firearms openly, and the Panthers took full advantage of that. They began patrolling their neighborhoods, watching the police, following them on their beats to ensure they didn't abuse their power.

When the police stopped someone, the Panthers were there, guns in hand, quoting the law to make sure no rights were violated.

It wasn't just about stopping individual acts of brutality—it was about creating a spectacle. When a squad of young Black men with rifles showed up to confront the police, the image was impossible to ignore. It was defiance made flesh, a statement that said: *we're not going to take this anymore.*

The Power of Presence

The Panthers understood the power of presence better than anyone. In a world where Black people were conditioned to be invisible, to keep their heads down and their mouths shut, the Panthers were a visual and physical challenge to the status quo.

Their uniforms—black leather jackets, black berets, and sunglasses—were as much a weapon as their guns. The look was militant, disciplined, and intimidating. It told the world that they were soldiers in a war for liberation.

And when they showed up—whether at a protest, a rally, or a courthouse—their presence changed everything. People listened. People paid attention.

In 1967, the Panthers made headlines when they marched on the California State Capitol in Sacramento, armed and unapologetic, to protest a proposed gun control law aimed at disarming them. It was a masterstroke of propaganda of the deed. The sight of armed Black men in the halls of government sent a message not just to California but to the entire country: *we're here, and we're not afraid.*

Guns and Groceries

But the Panthers weren't just about guns and confrontation. They understood that revolutionary action had to be about more than just fighting the system—it had to be about building something better.

One of the most remarkable aspects of the Black Panther Party was its community programs, which they called "Survival Programs."

The Panthers opened free breakfast programs for children, feeding tens of thousands of kids who might otherwise have gone hungry. They set up health clinics, offering free medical care and testing for diseases like sickle cell anemia, which disproportionately affected Black communities and had been largely ignored by the medical establishment.

They even created community patrols to escort the elderly and ensure their safety.

These programs weren't just charity—they were acts of defiance. They exposed the failures of the government and demonstrated that the Black community could take care of itself. Every meal served, every life saved, was a form of propaganda of the deed: a tangible reminder that the Panthers were building the world they wanted to see.

The FBI Strikes Back

Of course, none of this went unnoticed by the powers that be. J. Edgar Hoover, head of the FBI, famously declared the Black Panther Party "the greatest threat to the internal security of the United States."

The government launched a relentless campaign to destroy the Panthers, using its infamous COINTELPRO (Counter Intelligence Program). They infiltrated the organization, spread false rumors, and orchestrated arrests and assassinations.

One of the most notorious incidents was the killing of Fred Hampton, a charismatic young Panther leader in Chicago. In December 1969, police raided Hampton's apartment in the middle of the night, shooting him in his bed. It was a cold-blooded execution, orchestrated with FBI involvement.

But even in death, Hampton became a symbol. His assassination exposed the lengths to which the government would go to silence dissent, turning him into a martyr for the cause.

A Legacy of Resistance

By the early 1970s, the Black Panther Party was in decline, fractured by internal divisions and crushed under the weight of government repression. But their impact was undeniable.

The Panthers had shown the world what resistance looked like. They had taken the abstract ideals of justice, equality, and self-determination and turned them into something real, something you could see and touch.

Their legacy lives on, not just in the history books but in the movements they inspired. From Black Lives Matter to the fight for economic justice, the Panthers' spirit of defiance and self-reliance continues to resonate.

The Meaning of the Deed

The Black Panthers were more than a political party. They were a movement, a challenge, a symbol. Their actions—whether it was patrolling the streets with guns or feeding children breakfast—were deliberate acts of propaganda of the deed.

They didn't wait for permission or approval. They acted. And in doing so, they forced the world to reckon with the reality of systemic racism and oppression.

Their deeds sent a clear message: change doesn't come from asking nicely. It comes from standing up, from showing up, from making your presence felt in a way that can't be ignored.

And sometimes, that means picking up a gun. Sometimes, it means picking up a spatula.

Because in the end, it's not just about what you do. It's about what your actions say.

Chapter 10: Anti-Colonial Struggles

When it comes to tearing down empires, there's no neat formula. Some battles are fought with rifles in the jungle, others with hunger strikes in the streets. The weapons of choice—whether they're books, bombs, or bare hands—depend on who's fighting, who they're fighting against, and what they're fighting for.

Anti-colonial struggles are a study in contrasts. On one end of the spectrum, you have the serene, unshakable figure of Mahatma Gandhi, spinning thread on his charkha and preaching nonviolence. On the other, there's Frantz Fanon, his prose sharp enough to cut glass, telling the colonized masses that liberation will be born in fire and fury.

Both were warriors, though their weapons couldn't have been more different. And both understood the same fundamental truth: the act itself—the deed—is the thing. Whether it's holding a march or taking up arms, it's the action that speaks, the action that stirs people from their slumber and says, *Wake up. The time has come to fight.*

This chapter is about those fights, those deeds. It's about how Gandhi, Fanon, and countless others turned their actions into weapons against colonialism.

A World in Chains

To understand the deeds, you have to understand the chains. Colonialism wasn't just a political system; it was a theft of identity, a theft of soul. The colonizers didn't just take land—they took language, culture, dignity. They made the colonized believe they were less than human, that their place in the world was to serve, obey, and submit.

It was a prison without bars, a slow suffocation that made you forget what freedom even felt like. But some people never forgot.

From India to Algeria to Kenya to Vietnam, anti-colonial movements rose up to break the chains. Each one had its own context, its own strategy, its own heroes. But whether the struggle was waged with nonviolence or violence, the goal was always the same: to make the colonizer understand, in no uncertain terms, that their time was up.

Gandhi and the Power of Nonviolence

When Mohandas Karamchand Gandhi returned to India in 1915 after spending years in South Africa, he brought with him a weapon more potent than any rifle: *satyagraha*. It was a word he had coined, meaning "truth force" or "soul force," and it was the philosophy that would guide his fight against British colonial rule.

For Gandhi, action was essential—but not just any action. His deeds had to reflect his values, and his values were rooted in nonviolence.

The British Empire wasn't just an oppressor; it was a machine, cold and unfeeling. Its power came from control—of resources, of people, of narrative. Gandhi's genius was in recognizing that the best way to fight a machine wasn't with force but with refusal.

Refusal to cooperate. Refusal to obey. Refusal to play the part of the passive, submissive subject.

The Salt March

In 1930, Gandhi launched one of the most iconic acts of anti-colonial resistance: the Salt March. At the time, the British controlled the production and sale of salt in India, imposing a tax that hit the poor the hardest. Salt was a necessity, and the tax on it was a daily reminder of British domination.

So Gandhi walked.

For 24 days, he and a growing band of followers marched 240 miles to the Arabian Sea, where Gandhi bent down, scooped up a handful of salt, and broke the law. It was a small, almost laughably simple act, but its implications were seismic.

The Salt March was propaganda of the deed at its finest. It wasn't just about the salt—it was about showing the world that the British Empire could be defied. It was about inspiring millions of Indians to take similar actions, to see themselves as agents of change.

And it worked. The march sparked protests across the country, galvanizing the independence movement and forcing the

British to confront the fact that their rule was no longer uncontested.

The Limits of Nonviolence

But Gandhi's philosophy wasn't without its critics. Nonviolence required immense discipline, immense patience. It demanded that you endure beatings, imprisonment, and even death without striking back.

For some, that was too much to ask.

In the 1940s, as India edged closer to independence, more radical voices began to emerge. Subhas Chandra Bose, for example, rejected nonviolence outright, forming the Indian National Army to fight the British with weapons and military tactics.

Even within the independence movement, there was tension between those who believed in Gandhi's methods and those who thought that freedom couldn't be won without bloodshed.

This tension wasn't unique to India. Across the colonized world, the question loomed: to fight or to endure? To strike back or to hold the line?

Fanon and the Case for Violence

If Gandhi was the face of nonviolence, Frantz Fanon was its counterpoint. Born in Martinique, Fanon was a psychiatrist, writer, and revolutionary who became one of the most influential voices in the fight against colonialism.

Fanon's most famous work, *The Wretched of the Earth,* is a searing indictment of colonialism and a call to arms for the oppressed. For Fanon, violence wasn't just a necessary evil in the struggle for liberation—it was a cleansing force, a way for the colonized to reclaim their humanity.

"Violence," he wrote, "frees the native from his inferiority complex and from his despair and inaction; it makes him fearless and restores his self-respect."

Fanon's ideas were born out of his experiences in Algeria, where the National Liberation Front (FLN) waged a bloody war against French colonial rule.

The Algerian War of Independence

The Algerian War, which lasted from 1954 to 1962, was one of the most brutal anti-colonial struggles of the 20th century. The FLN used guerrilla tactics, planting bombs in cafes and ambushing French soldiers. The French, in turn, responded with torture, mass arrests, and scorched-earth campaigns.

For Fanon, the violence wasn't just a means to an end—it was part of the process of decolonization. To him, the colonized had been stripped of their agency, their sense of self, by years of oppression. Violence was a way to reclaim it, to assert their right to exist as free people.

But it came at a cost. The war left deep scars on both sides, and even after Algeria won its independence, the trauma lingered.

Comparing the Approaches

Gandhi and Fanon represent two sides of the same coin. Both understood that colonialism wasn't just a political or economic system—it was a psychological one. It was about control, about making the colonized believe they were powerless.

Their methods, however, couldn't have been more different.

Gandhi believed in appealing to the oppressor's conscience, in using nonviolence to expose the moral bankruptcy of colonialism. Fanon, on the other hand, believed that liberation could only be achieved through confrontation, through an unapologetic assertion of power.

Which approach was more effective? That depends on the context. In India, Gandhi's nonviolence worked because it exposed the contradictions of British rule. In Algeria, the French were too entrenched, too brutal, for nonviolence to succeed.

The Deed as Message

What unites Gandhi and Fanon, despite their differences, is their understanding of the power of action. Whether it's breaking a law or breaking a chain, the deed itself is the message.

For Gandhi, the Salt March was a way to show Indians that they could resist, that they didn't need to rely on the British for something as basic as salt. For Fanon, the FLN's guerrilla tactics were a way to show the French that their time in Algeria was over, that they could no longer rule without consequence.

In both cases, the actions were symbolic as much as they were practical. They were about more than just achieving a specific goal—they were about inspiring a movement, shaking people awake, and forcing the world to pay attention.

The Legacy of Anti-Colonial Struggles

The fight against colonialism didn't end with Gandhi or Fanon. Their ideas and methods have echoed through history, influencing movements from South Africa to Palestine to the Americas.

And the question they grappled with—nonviolence or violence, patience or confrontation—is one that every struggle for justice must confront.

What they both understood, though, is that the status quo doesn't change on its own. It takes action. It takes courage. It takes a deed.

Because in the end, it's not just about what you fight against. It's about what you fight for.

Chapter 11: Environmental Direct Action

The Earth has been screaming for centuries. It's not the kind of scream you hear all at once, not a shriek of terror like you'd find in a horror flick, but a low, mournful wail, stretched across decades. The glaciers are weeping, the forests are choking, the seas are boiling. If you listen closely—really closely—you can hear it. Most people can't, or won't.

But some people, they not only hear the Earth's scream, they feel it, like a knife twisting in their gut. And they don't just sit there clutching their stomachs. They act.

This chapter is about those people—the ones who refuse to go quietly while the planet burns around them. Environmental direct action has become a potent form of propaganda of the deed in the modern era, blending urgency, theatricality, and symbolism to wake the world up to the climate crisis.

From the radical tactics of the Earth Liberation Front (ELF) to the coordinated mass disruptions of Extinction Rebellion (XR), environmental direct action isn't just about saving the planet. It's about forcing people to look at what we've done and what we stand to lose.

A Fight Against the Apocalypse

PROPAGANDA OF THE DEED

Let's not sugarcoat it: the stakes in this fight are higher than they've ever been. We're talking about the survival of life as we know it. Climate change, deforestation, species extinction, ocean acidification—pick your poison. The facts are as grim as the gloomiest of Stephen King novels, except this isn't fiction.

Governments and corporations have been warned for decades. Scientists have sounded alarms. Reports have been published, protests held, promises made. And yet, here we are, teetering on the edge of catastrophe.

This is where environmental direct action comes in. It's not about politely asking for change. It's about demanding it, with actions so bold, so disruptive, that they're impossible to ignore.

The Earth Liberation Front: Guerrillas in the Shadows

If there's a villain in the environmental movement—or at least a group painted as villains—it's the Earth Liberation Front, or ELF. Born in the 1990s in the Pacific Northwest, the ELF was a decentralized network of eco-saboteurs. Their mission? To stop environmental destruction by any means necessary.

For the ELF, talk wasn't enough. Petitions, protests, letters to the editor—those were fine for people who believed in playing by the rules. But the ELF didn't believe in those rules.

Their methods were dramatic, to say the least: arson, vandalism, sabotage. They burned down luxury housing developments, torched SUV dealerships, and destroyed equipment used for logging and mining.

It was all about sending a message. The developers, the oil companies, the timber corporations—they were the villains in the ELF's story, and the fires were their way of saying, *We see you. We will not let you destroy this planet without a fight.*

But it wasn't just about destruction. The ELF took great care to avoid harming people. They weren't terrorists, at least not in their own eyes. They were warriors, fighting for a cause bigger than themselves.

Symbolism in Flames

The ELF's actions weren't random acts of violence. They were meticulously planned, each one designed to make a point. When they burned down a ski resort expansion in Vail, Colorado, in 1998, it wasn't just about the resort—it was about the habitat of the endangered lynx that the expansion threatened to destroy.

When they targeted Hummers and other gas-guzzling SUVs, it wasn't just about the cars—it was about the culture of consumerism and waste they represented.

These acts were propaganda of the deed in its purest form. They weren't meant to solve the problem overnight. They were meant to spark conversation, to force people to confront the environmental destruction happening all around them.

Of course, the ELF's tactics were controversial. To some, they were heroes, willing to take risks that others wouldn't. To others, they were criminals, their methods counterproductive and their message lost in the smoke and flames.

Extinction Rebellion: Disrupt and Inspire

If the ELF was the shadowy vigilante of the environmental movement, Extinction Rebellion is its theater troupe. Founded in the UK in 2018, XR takes a different approach to direct action—one that's less about sabotage and more about spectacle.

XR's philosophy is rooted in nonviolent civil disobedience. Their goal is to disrupt the status quo, not with flames, but with creativity and sheer numbers. They block roads, occupy buildings, and stage elaborate performances to draw attention to the climate crisis.

And they do it all with a flair for the dramatic. Protesters have dressed as ghosts, as blood-soaked corpses, as bees. They've glued themselves to government buildings, chained themselves to bridges, and even poured fake blood onto the steps of the Treasury in London.

Each action is a performance, designed to grab headlines and stir emotions.

The Art of Disruption

XR's strength lies in its ability to disrupt daily life. When protesters block a major road or shut down an airport, it forces people to stop and take notice. It creates inconvenience, yes, but that inconvenience is the point.

The message is simple: if we don't take drastic action to address the climate crisis, the disruptions caused by protests will pale in comparison to the disruptions caused by a collapsing ecosystem.

It's not just about drawing attention—it's about creating a sense of urgency. XR wants people to feel the crisis in their bones, to understand that this isn't a problem for the future. It's happening now.

A Global Movement

What sets XR apart is its global reach. From London to New York to Sydney, XR chapters have sprung up around the world, each one adapting the movement's tactics to its local context.

In 2019, XR staged a two-week-long protest in London, blocking major intersections and landmarks. The action brought the city to a standstill and dominated the headlines, forcing the UK government to declare a climate emergency.

But XR's methods haven't been without criticism. Some argue that their actions alienate people rather than inspire them, that the disruption they create only fuels resentment.

It's a fine line to walk—being disruptive enough to make an impact, but not so much that you lose public support.

The Role of Symbolism

Whether it's the ELF's fires or XR's performances, symbolism is at the heart of environmental direct action. These acts aren't just about the immediate impact—they're about what they represent.

A tree spiked by an eco-saboteur isn't just a tree. It's a statement about defiance, about the value of the natural world over profit. A protester superglued to a building isn't just a nuisance. They're a living embodiment of the urgency of the climate crisis.

These actions force people to confront the reality of what's happening, to see the destruction in a way that can't be ignored or dismissed.

Ethics and Effectiveness

Of course, not everyone agrees on the ethics or effectiveness of these methods. The ELF's arsons, for example, were often condemned for their potential to escalate into violence. XR's disruptions, meanwhile, have been criticized for alienating the very people they're trying to persuade.

But the question remains: what's the alternative? Polite letters to politicians? Recycling more plastic bottles? Those things might make people feel good, but they won't stop a pipeline from being built or a rainforest from being razed.

For many in the environmental movement, the urgency of the crisis justifies the risk of alienation, the risk of backlash. They believe that when the stakes are this high, you have to be willing to make people uncomfortable.

The Future of Environmental Direct Action

As the climate crisis worsens, the methods of environmental direct action will likely evolve. New groups will emerge, new tactics will be tried, and the debate over how far is too far will continue.

But one thing is certain: the Earth's scream isn't going to stop. And as long as there are people who can hear it, there will be those who act.

Because in the end, that's what propaganda of the deed is all about. It's not just about changing the world—it's about refusing to let the world stay the same. It's about standing up, taking a risk, and saying, *Enough.*

The Earth needs fighters, dreamers, and doers. It needs people willing to light a fire—whether it's a literal one or the kind that burns in the heart.

Chapter 12: 9/11 and the Dark Side of Propaganda of the Deed

Terror has a peculiar weight to it. It isn't the kind of weight you can hold in your hand or put on a scale. It's the invisible kind, the oppressive force that fills the air after something unspeakable happens. And on September 11, 2001, the air was thick with it.

The planes hit, and the towers fell. First one, then the other, crumbling into clouds of ash, steel, and shattered lives. For a moment, the entire world seemed to stop breathing. It was an act that burned itself into the collective consciousness of humanity, as much a symbol as it was a tragedy.

9/11 wasn't just an attack. It was a message, written in fire and blood across the New York skyline. And for better or worse, it represented the darkest potential of propaganda of the deed—a concept twisted beyond recognition into something monstrous.

This chapter explores the hijacking of propaganda of the deed by extremist groups like al-Qaeda, who used the same principles that revolutionaries and freedom fighters had wielded for liberation—but warped them into tools of terror.

The Anatomy of a Nightmare

To understand 9/11 as propaganda of the deed, you have to strip away, for a moment, the raw emotion of the event. Not the grief—that lingers in the marrow of anyone who remembers that day—but the noise, the talking heads, the conspiracy theories, and the politics. Look at it from a cold, calculating perspective.

What was al-Qaeda trying to achieve?

The immediate goal was destruction—of buildings, lives, and the illusion of invulnerability in the United States. But the real objective was symbolic. The Twin Towers weren't just buildings; they were icons of American economic power. The Pentagon wasn't just an office complex; it was the nerve center of U.S. military might.

By targeting these symbols, al-Qaeda sent a message to the world: even the mightiest nation on Earth could bleed. It was propaganda of the deed, intended not to spark a revolution, but to sow chaos, fear, and distrust on a global scale.

A Twisted Manifesto

Propaganda of the deed is, at its core, about communication. It's about using actions—not words—to convey a message so visceral, so undeniable, that it forces people to pay attention.

Historically, this concept had been used by anarchists, suffragettes, and revolutionaries to challenge oppressive systems and inspire change. The act itself was a tool, a way to force the world to confront injustice.

But 9/11 flipped the script. Instead of liberation, the message was subjugation. Instead of hope, it carried despair. Al-Qaeda exploited the same principles of dramatic action and symbolic resonance, but they did it in service of fear and fanaticism.

In their eyes, the attack was a kind of grotesque performance, designed to provoke not just a response, but an overreaction. They wanted the U.S. to lash out, to embroil itself in endless wars, to drain its resources and fracture its alliances.

And in many ways, they succeeded.

The Dark Mirror of Revolutionary Action

If propaganda of the deed is about igniting a spark, then 9/11 was an inferno. But the flame it lit wasn't one of righteous anger or hope for a better world. It was one of fear, mistrust, and division.

Think back to the roots of the concept, to figures like Carlo Pisacane or Mikhail Bakunin. For them, the deed was supposed to inspire solidarity, to rally the oppressed against their oppressors. Even when violence was involved, it was framed as a means to an end—a better, freer society.

Al-Qaeda took that same framework and stripped it of its ethical core. They didn't care about solidarity; they thrived on division. They didn't aim for liberation; they reveled in destruction.

It's a dark reminder of how powerful ideas can be co-opted, twisted, and weaponized. The same tools that had once been used to fight for justice were now being wielded to spread terror.

The Media: Amplifiers of Fear

Propaganda of the deed relies on visibility. An act, no matter how dramatic, is meaningless if no one sees it. And in the age of 24-hour news and global media networks, al-Qaeda understood this better than anyone.

The images of 9/11 were broadcast around the world in real time. The planes hitting the towers, the smoke billowing into the sky, the buildings collapsing into a hellish cloud of debris—it was all there, playing on an endless loop.

This wasn't an accident. Al-Qaeda knew that the media would become an unwitting accomplice, amplifying their message far beyond what they could have achieved on their own. The attacks weren't just a strike against America; they were a psychological assault on the entire world.

The coverage turned the event into a shared trauma, a spectacle of horror that transcended borders. It created a narrative of vulnerability and fear, one that would shape global politics for decades to come.

Collateral Damage: The Global Fallout

The true horror of 9/11 wasn't just the lives lost on that day—it was the chain reaction it set off. Wars in Afghanistan and Iraq. A surge in Islamophobia. The erosion of civil liberties in the name of security.

PROPAGANDA OF THE DEED

The U.S. government's response to 9/11 was exactly what al-Qaeda had hoped for: a massive, militarized overreach. The War on Terror became a black hole, sucking in trillions of dollars, countless lives, and the moral standing of nations involved.

Meanwhile, the world became a more divided place. Trust between nations eroded. Extremism flourished, feeding off the chaos. The scars of 9/11 weren't just physical or emotional—they were geopolitical, reshaping the global landscape in ways that are still being felt today.

The Ethics of Fear

What makes 9/11 such a chilling example of propaganda of the deed is its sheer cynicism. At its heart, the concept is supposed to be about hope—about using dramatic action to inspire people to believe in the possibility of change.

But 9/11 was never about hope. It was about fear. It was about taking the tools of revolution and using them to terrorize, manipulate, and divide.

And yet, it worked. The world did change. Not in the way al-Qaeda envisioned—there was no grand uprising against Western powers, no sweeping wave of Islamic fundamentalism—but in ways that were arguably even more profound.

The question, then, is what this says about propaganda of the deed itself. Is it inherently neutral, a tool that can be used for good or evil? Or does its reliance on shock and spectacle make it vulnerable to exploitation by those with darker agendas?

Lessons from the Abyss

If there's anything to be learned from 9/11, it's this: the power of symbolic action is a double-edged sword. It can inspire or it can terrorize. It can liberate or it can oppress.

The key difference lies in intent. Are you fighting for justice, or are you sowing chaos? Are you aiming to uplift, or to destroy?

For those who believe in the potential of propaganda of the deed to create positive change, 9/11 is a cautionary tale. It's a reminder of what happens when the ethical core of the concept is abandoned, when the deed becomes an end in itself rather than a means to something greater.

A World Changed Forever

In the years since 9/11, the world has grappled with the aftermath of that dark day. The scars are still there, visible in the geopolitical tensions, the rise of surveillance states, and the ongoing threat of extremism.

But perhaps the most lasting legacy of 9/11 is the way it reshaped our understanding of propaganda of the deed. It showed us its potential—not just for liberation, but for devastation. It reminded us that actions have power, but that power can be wielded for good or ill.

In the end, 9/11 was a turning point, not just for the world, but for the concept of propaganda of the deed itself. It forced us to confront its darkest possibilities, to reckon with the consequences of actions designed to shock, provoke, and terrify.

And it left us with a question: how do we reclaim this tool from the darkness? How do we ensure that the deeds we choose to carry out are ones that build, rather than destroy?

That's a question for the next chapter. For now, let's sit with the weight of what 9/11 taught us: that even the most powerful ideas can be twisted, and that the line between inspiration and terror is thinner than we'd like to admit.

Chapter 13: The Power of Symbolism

Actions speak louder than words, or so the old saying goes. But the truth is, actions don't just speak—they shout, they echo, and sometimes they sing. When an act strikes the right chord, it becomes more than just a thing that happened. It becomes a symbol. And symbols, as we've seen time and time again, have the power to change the world.

Think about the way a single image can haunt your mind for days. The photo of a lone man standing in front of a tank in Tiananmen Square. The shot of a barefoot child fleeing napalm in Vietnam. The smoldering Twin Towers collapsing into dust. These aren't just snapshots—they're symbols, frozen moments of history that carry a weight far heavier than their individual parts.

In this chapter, we'll explore why symbolism is so potent, how it resonates in the collective imagination, and how it can spark cultural shifts that ripple across time and space. But be warned: the power of symbolism is a double-edged sword. Like fire, it can illuminate or destroy. It all depends on who's holding the match.

The Anatomy of a Symbol

A symbol, at its most basic level, is a stand-in. It takes something physical—a gesture, an object, an act—and layers it with meaning. It's shorthand for an idea, a feeling, a movement. The clenched fist raised high is more than just a fist; it's defiance, solidarity, and power. A toppled statue isn't just a lump of bronze; it's the crumbling of an old order, the rewriting of a narrative.

The most powerful symbols don't come from a boardroom or a branding agency. They're born in the wild, in moments of raw, unscripted humanity. They arise when someone does something so brave, or shocking, or heart-wrenching that it transcends the act itself.

Take Rosa Parks. When she refused to give up her seat on that Montgomery bus, she wasn't thinking about symbolism. She was tired. But that single act of defiance became a symbol, not just for the civil rights movement, but for the universal struggle against oppression.

The key to a symbol's power lies in its ability to resonate. It has to strike a nerve, to tap into something deeply felt but not always articulated. A symbol doesn't just represent an idea; it brings that idea to life.

How Actions Become Symbols

So, how does an action move from being something that happens to being something that matters? It's not magic, although it can feel like it. There's a process—a kind of alchemy—that turns deeds into symbols.

1. **Context Is Everything**
   The same action can mean wildly different things

depending on when and where it happens. A man setting himself on fire might seem like a senseless tragedy. But when Mohamed Bouazizi, a Tunisian street vendor, did it in 2010, it became the spark for the Arab Spring. Why? Because his act tapped into a collective frustration with corruption, inequality, and repression.

2. **Simplicity and Clarity**

Symbols work best when they're easy to understand. Think of the Berlin Wall. Its fall in 1989 wasn't just a physical event; it was a clear, visceral representation of the collapse of communism and the end of an era.

3. **Emotional Impact**

A good symbol doesn't just make you think—it makes you feel. It stirs something primal. When the suffragettes smashed windows and chained themselves to fences, it wasn't just about the act itself. It was the rage, the desperation, the sheer refusal to be ignored that made those deeds resonate.

4. **Amplification**

An action only becomes a symbol if people know about it. That's where the media, the internet, and good old-fashioned word of mouth come in. A protest in a small town might seem like a drop in the ocean, but if the right photo goes viral, it can turn into a tidal wave.

The Resonance of Symbols

Symbols don't just stick around—they grow. They evolve. They become part of our collective consciousness, passed down like heirlooms.

Think of the Guy Fawkes mask. Originally tied to a failed plot to blow up the English Parliament, it was resurrected in *V for Vendetta*, then adopted by hacktivist groups like Anonymous. Today, it's a symbol of resistance against tyranny, even though most people wearing it couldn't tell you much about Guy Fawkes himself.

Or consider the rainbow flag. When Gilbert Baker first designed it in 1978, it was just a piece of cloth. But over time, it became a global symbol of LGBTQ+ pride and rights. It doesn't matter if you're in San Francisco or Singapore—when you see that flag, you know what it stands for.

This is the magic of symbols: they take on lives of their own. They become bigger than the people or events that created them.

When Symbols Spark Movements

The power of a symbol isn't just in its ability to resonate—it's in its ability to mobilize. A powerful symbol can turn apathy into action, outrage into organization.

Take the black-and-white photo of Emmett Till, the 14-year-old boy lynched in Mississippi in 1955. His mother, Mamie Till-Mobley, insisted on an open-casket funeral so the world could see what had been done to her son. The image of his mutilated body became a rallying cry for the civil rights movement, galvanizing a nation to confront its own horrors.

Or think about Greta Thunberg, the Swedish teenager who sat outside her parliament with a sign that read "School Strike for Climate." It was such a simple act, but it struck a chord. That one sign became a global movement, with millions of young people demanding action on climate change.

Symbols don't just reflect the world—they shape it. They create momentum, draw lines in the sand, and give people something to rally around.

The Dangers of Symbolism

But here's the thing about symbols: they're slippery. They can be co-opted, distorted, and weaponized.

The Confederate flag, for example, started as a battle flag in the Civil War. For some, it's a symbol of heritage. For others, it's a symbol of hate. The same piece of cloth carries wildly different meanings depending on who's waving it and why.

Or think about the swastika. For centuries, it was a symbol of good fortune in many cultures. Then the Nazis got hold of it, and now it's forever tied to one of the darkest chapters in human history.

Symbols are powerful because they're malleable. But that malleability is also what makes them dangerous.

The Future of Symbolism

In the digital age, symbols are evolving faster than ever. A hashtag can become a rallying cry. A meme can become a political statement. The Black Lives Matter movement, for example, started as a simple phrase. But over time, it became a global symbol of the fight against racial injustice.

And yet, the speed of modern communication comes with its own risks. Symbols can rise and fall in the blink of an eye. They can be diluted, commercialized, or forgotten.

The challenge, then, is to create symbols that endure. Symbols that don't just resonate in the moment, but that have the power to inspire long-term change.

The Weight of Meaning

Symbols are more than just ideas made visible. They're vessels for our hopes, our fears, and our dreams. They're how we make sense of the world, how we tell our stories, and how we shape the future.

But with great power comes great responsibility. When you create a symbol—when you perform an act that you hope will resonate—you're not just making a statement. You're creating something that could outlive you, something that could inspire or terrify generations to come.

The power of symbolism lies in its ability to connect us, to move us, to push us toward something greater. But it's up to us to decide what that something is. Will we use this power to build, or to destroy?

That choice, like all meaningful choices, is ours to make. And the weight of it is heavier than any symbol could ever convey.

Chapter 14: A Catalyst for Change

Change doesn't come gently. It doesn't tiptoe in wearing slippers, speaking in whispers. No, real change is a freight train that barrels through the silence, shattering the glass houses of comfort and apathy. For oppressed populations, change often feels less like an invitation and more like a demand—a stark, sudden shift in the landscape of what's possible. And at the heart of these transformations, you'll find something remarkable: a radical deed that struck the match.

This chapter dives deep into the anatomy of that catalytic moment. It's not about polite negotiations or incremental reforms; it's about the raw, undeniable energy of actions that rip through the status quo. These deeds, whether acts of defiance, protest, or rebellion, force people to look, think, and—most importantly—act. They disrupt complacency, ignite outrage, and set the wheels of history in motion.

The Nature of Complacency

Before we talk about the catalyst, we need to understand the problem it disrupts: complacency. Oppression is like a heavy fog; it settles in slowly, dulling the senses and obscuring the horizon. People learn to live with it because resisting seems futile, and the alternative—fighting back—is terrifying. Over time, the unacceptable becomes normal.

Complacency isn't just about laziness or indifference. It's a survival mechanism. If you're an oppressed worker in a factory, or a woman denied the right to vote, or a Black teenager living under Jim Crow, raising your voice can get you fired, ostracized, or killed. So, you keep your head down. You endure.

But here's the thing about complacency: it's brittle. On the surface, it looks solid, like a calm lake. But beneath that stillness is a deep well of frustration, anger, and longing. All it takes is one stone thrown into the water to break the surface tension. That's what a radical deed does—it smashes the calm and sends ripples out in every direction.

The Anatomy of a Catalyst

What makes a deed catalytic? It's not just the action itself, though that's important. It's the way the act taps into the collective psyche of the oppressed, awakening something that's been lying dormant.

1. **It Forces a Reckoning**
    A catalytic deed makes it impossible to ignore the problem. When Rosa Parks refused to give up her seat, it wasn't just about one woman on one bus. It was about the entire system of segregation that her act exposed. Suddenly, the world couldn't look away.
2. **It Feels Personal**
    A powerful deed connects on a visceral level. It's not an abstract argument or a dry policy debate—it's raw and real. When the suffragettes smashed shop windows in London, it wasn't just property damage.

It was a cry of rage, a demand to be seen and heard.

3. **It Creates Momentum**

   A single act can set off a chain reaction. Think of the Stonewall Riots in 1969. What started as a spontaneous act of defiance against police harassment turned into a tipping point for the LGBTQ+ rights movement.

4. **It Offers a Glimpse of Possibility**

   A catalytic deed shows that change isn't just a dream—it's within reach. When enslaved people in the United States heard about Nat Turner's rebellion, it wasn't just a story of violence; it was a spark of hope, a reminder that resistance was possible.

From Outrage to Action

A radical deed doesn't just disrupt complacency; it inspires action. But inspiration is a tricky thing. It's not enough to stir the pot—you need to keep it boiling.

Take the Montgomery Bus Boycott, for example. Rosa Parks' arrest was the catalyst, but the boycott itself was the movement. For over a year, Black residents of Montgomery refused to ride the buses, organizing carpools and walking miles to work. It was a massive, sustained effort that required discipline and sacrifice. But it worked.

Or look at the Indian independence movement. Gandhi's Salt March in 1930 was a symbolic act of defiance, a rejection of British authority over something as basic as salt. But the real power lay in what followed: millions of Indians joined the campaign, breaking colonial laws and demanding self-rule.

The key is transformation. A deed disrupts the status quo, but a movement builds something new in its place.

The Risks of Radical Action

Of course, not every catalytic deed leads to positive change. Sometimes, the disruption is met with backlash. Sometimes, the momentum fizzles out. And sometimes, the deed is co-opted or misinterpreted, turning its message into a weapon for the very forces it sought to challenge.

The Haymarket Affair in 1886 is a prime example. What began as a peaceful rally for workers' rights turned into a violent clash when a bomb exploded, killing police officers and protesters alike. The incident became a pretext for a crackdown on labor activists, with several anarchists executed despite flimsy evidence.

Or consider the assassination of Archduke Franz Ferdinand in 1914. The deed was meant to strike a blow against Austro-Hungarian imperialism, but it triggered World War I—a conflict that brought unprecedented destruction and left much of Europe in ruins.

The lesson here is that radical deeds are unpredictable. They can inspire, but they can also provoke fear and repression. The stakes are always high.

Case Study: The Catalysts of the Civil Rights Movement

PROPAGANDA OF THE DEED

The civil rights movement in the United States is a masterclass in the power of catalytic deeds. Each act of defiance, each protest, each sit-in was a stone thrown into the water, creating ripples that grew into waves.

- **The Greensboro Sit-Ins (1960):** Four Black college students sat down at a whites-only lunch counter in North Carolina and refused to leave. Their quiet, dignified resistance sparked a wave of sit-ins across the South, challenging segregation in a way that couldn't be ignored.

- **The Freedom Rides (1961):** Integrated groups of activists rode buses through the Deep South, testing desegregation laws and facing brutal violence along the way. Their courage forced the federal government to confront the reality of Jim Crow.

- **The March on Washington (1963):** A quarter of a million people gathered on the National Mall, demanding jobs and freedom. The sheer scale of the march, combined with Martin Luther King Jr.'s iconic "I Have a Dream" speech, made it impossible to deny the urgency of the movement.

Each of these deeds was more than just an event—it was a turning point, a moment when the tide of history shifted.

The Double-Edged Sword of Hope

Hope is the lifeblood of any movement, but it's also a dangerous thing. It can sustain people through hardship, but it can also lead to despair if change doesn't come quickly enough.

This is why catalytic deeds need to be followed by concrete action. A symbol, no matter how powerful, is not enough on its own. The real work lies in building the infrastructure of change—organizing, educating, and mobilizing.

But even when progress is slow, the memory of a catalytic deed can keep hope alive. It's a reminder that the status quo is not immutable, that the world can be shaken and remade.

The Spark and the Fire

A catalytic deed is like a spark in a dry forest. It's sudden, it's dramatic, and it demands attention. But a spark alone isn't enough to create a wildfire. You need fuel, oxygen, and time.

The fuel is the collective frustration of the oppressed, the deep well of anger and longing that lies beneath the surface. The oxygen is the attention of the world, the amplification of the deed's message through media and storytelling. And the time? Well, that's the hardest part. Change doesn't happen overnight. It's a slow burn, but once it starts, it's hard to stop.

Radical deeds disrupt complacency, yes. But their true power lies in what they ignite: a fire of action, of resistance, of possibility. For those living under the weight of oppression, that fire is more than a metaphor—it's survival, it's hope, it's the promise of a better world.

PROPAGANDA OF THE DEED

And sometimes, all it takes to light the flame is one bold, defiant act. One spark in the darkness. One catalyst for change.

Chapter 15: Addressing Criticism

Criticism is a tricky beast. It comes at you in all shapes and sizes—sometimes a sharp knife, sometimes a dull club, sometimes a whisper in your ear that you can't quite shake. When it comes to propaganda of the deed, the critiques aren't just annoying gnats buzzing around your head. They're full-on attacks, aimed at dismantling the very premise of why you would act boldly, dramatically, and unapologetically in the first place.

So, let's face the music. Let's walk straight into the lion's den of objections and come out the other side alive. Because if there's one thing we know about history, it's that bold action always has its detractors. The armchair critics, the cynics, the gatekeepers—they've been around forever, and they'll be here long after we're gone. But that doesn't mean they're right.

Criticism #1: "It's Ineffective"

The first and loudest critique is simple: *What's the point?* Detractors argue that propaganda of the deed doesn't work. They'll say it's all smoke and mirrors, dramatic gestures that fizzle out before they make any real impact.

Let's tear that apart.

History is brimming with examples of deeds that were dismissed as pointless at the time but later proved transformative. When Rosa Parks refused to give up her seat in 1955, plenty of people thought it was just a minor act of defiance. After all, it didn't dismantle segregation overnight. But that single moment became a flashpoint for the Montgomery Bus Boycott, which in turn catalyzed the broader civil rights movement.

The key here is to understand what "effective" means. Propaganda of the deed isn't always about immediate results. It's not a magic wand that solves systemic problems in one swoop. Instead, it's about planting a seed, sparking a conversation, and shifting the Overton window of what's possible. It's about breaking through the noise and making people pay attention.

Critics who demand instant results often miss the point. They're like someone standing over a sapling, tapping their foot impatiently, wondering why it isn't a towering oak tree yet. But oak trees take time. Movements take time. And propaganda of the deed is the spark that sets those movements in motion.

Criticism #2: "It Alienates the Masses"

Another common argument is that radical action scares people off. Critics claim that bold deeds—especially when they're disruptive or confrontational—alienate potential allies and push the broader public toward apathy or outright hostility.

Here's the thing: nobody ever changed the world by being universally liked.

Look at the suffragettes. In the early 20th century, they were accused of being hysterical, violent, and unreasonable.

Newspapers mocked them, politicians condemned them, and plenty of ordinary people thought they were going too far. And yet, their militancy forced the issue of women's suffrage into the spotlight. They made it impossible to ignore.

The truth is, bold action isn't supposed to make everyone comfortable. It's supposed to shake people out of their complacency. Yes, some will be alienated—that's inevitable. But the people who matter, the ones who are ready to take action or are on the cusp of awakening, will be inspired.

Social movements are not popularity contests. They're battles for justice, and battles are messy. If your first priority is winning over everyone, including your oppressors, you're already losing.

Criticism #3: "It's Counterproductive"

This critique is a close cousin of the alienation argument, but it has a darker edge. Critics say that propaganda of the deed doesn't just fail to help—it actively makes things worse. They point to examples where bold actions led to crackdowns, increased repression, or backlash against the very cause they sought to promote.

It's a fair concern. History isn't short on examples where bold deeds had unintended consequences. The Haymarket Affair of 1886 is a case in point. After the bombing and subsequent trial, labor activists faced a wave of repression, and the anarchist movement in the U.S. never fully recovered.

But here's the counterpoint: every struggle involves risk. There's no such thing as a cost-free revolution.

The question isn't whether bold action invites backlash—it almost always does. The question is whether the action is worth the risk. And more often than not, the answer is yes.

Take the Civil Rights Movement. The Freedom Rides of 1961 provoked brutal violence from segregationists, but that violence was broadcast on national television, forcing the federal government to intervene. The brutality didn't weaken the movement; it strengthened it, exposing the moral bankruptcy of the system and galvanizing support.

Propaganda of the deed isn't about avoiding backlash. It's about using that backlash to reveal the truth, to force the world to confront the injustice that the deed exposes.

Criticism #4: "It's Too Violent"

One of the most polarizing critiques of propaganda of the deed is its association with violence. Critics argue that violent acts—whether assassinations, bombings, or riots—are inherently unjustifiable, regardless of the cause. They'll say that violence alienates people, invites repression, and undermines the moral high ground.

Let's not sugarcoat it: violence is a slippery slope. It's dangerous, unpredictable, and morally fraught. But to dismiss it outright is to ignore the complexities of history.

When enslaved people revolted against their masters, was that unjustifiable violence? When colonized nations fought back against imperial powers, were they supposed to do so politely?

Frantz Fanon, the anti-colonial thinker, argued that violence isn't just a tool—it's a language. For the oppressed, it's often the only language the oppressor understands. That doesn't mean violence should be glorified or used recklessly, but it does mean we need to think critically about the context in which it occurs.

Nonviolence has its power, no doubt. Gandhi's salt march and Martin Luther King Jr.'s peaceful protests changed the world. But to dismiss all forms of violent resistance as counterproductive or immoral is to ignore the realities of oppression.

The key is intentionality. Propaganda of the deed, whether violent or nonviolent, must be strategic. It must serve a purpose beyond the act itself, and it must aim to inspire rather than terrorize.

Criticism #5: "It's Just Self-Indulgent Theater"

This one stings. Critics will sneer that propaganda of the deed is nothing more than performative activism—a way for radicals to feel important without actually achieving anything. They'll point to activists chaining themselves to trees or storming corporate offices and say, "What did that actually accomplish?"

The accusation of theater isn't entirely wrong. Propaganda of the deed *is* theatrical. It's meant to grab attention, to create a spectacle that forces people to look. But here's the twist: theater isn't a bad thing. In fact, it's essential.

Think about the Boston Tea Party. Was it performative? Absolutely. A group of colonists dressed up as Mohawk Indians and dumped tea into the harbor. It was pure symbolism. But that symbolism ignited a revolution.

Theatrics, when done right, can cut through the noise and leave an indelible mark on the collective imagination. They can make people feel something—anger, hope, urgency—and that feeling is the first step toward action.

The problem isn't theater. The problem is empty theater—gestures with no strategy behind them. Effective propaganda of the deed combines spectacle with substance. It's not about ego; it's about impact.

Criticism #6: "It's Outdated"

Finally, some critics argue that propaganda of the deed is a relic of the past. They'll say that in an age of social media and digital activism, dramatic actions are unnecessary. Why stage a sit-in when you can start a hashtag? Why risk your life when you can raise awareness from the safety of your home?

It's a tempting argument, but it falls flat.

Social media is a powerful tool, no doubt. It amplifies voices, spreads information, and connects people across the globe. But digital activism alone isn't enough. A tweet can spark a conversation, but it can't blockade a pipeline. A hashtag can raise awareness, but it can't physically occupy a government building.

The truth is, we need both. Digital tools can amplify the message, but the message itself still needs to be rooted in action. Propaganda of the deed remains relevant because it does something social media can't: it creates a tangible, undeniable disruption.

The Critic and the Catalyst

Criticism will always be there, lurking in the shadows, waiting to pounce. And that's not a bad thing. Criticism forces us to think, to refine our strategies, to question our assumptions. But it shouldn't paralyze us. It shouldn't stop us from acting.

Propaganda of the deed isn't perfect. It's messy, risky, and often misunderstood. But it's also powerful. It's the match that lights the fire, the stone that breaks the surface tension, the spark that sets history in motion.

So, let the critics talk. Let them dissect, debate, and dismiss. Meanwhile, the doers—the ones who aren't afraid to act boldly, dramatically, and unapologetically—will keep changing the world. One deed at a time.

Chapter 16: Lessons from Successes and Failures

Propaganda of the deed is like a haunted mansion, full of secret doors and treacherous staircases. You step into it, hoping for revelation, but if you're not careful, you might end up falling through a trapdoor into a pit of failure. The question isn't whether it works—it's how and why it works when it does, and why it crashes and burns when it doesn't.

The thing about bold actions is that they're unpredictable. They can light the world on fire or blow up in your face, and sometimes, they do both at once. To understand the anatomy of propaganda of the deed, we have to dissect its successes and failures, peeling back the layers to uncover the bones of what works—and what doesn't.

So, grab your scalpel. It's time to get messy.

The Anatomy of Success

Let's start with the glittering examples, the stories where propaganda of the deed achieved its goals, inspiring movements, shifting public opinion, and carving its name into the annals of history. These are the moments that remind us why bold action matters.

1. Clear and Resonant Messaging

Success begins with a crystal-clear message. It's not enough to act boldly; you have to act with purpose, and that purpose must be obvious to the people watching. The deed itself should communicate your intent without a word being spoken.

Take the Greensboro sit-ins of 1960. Four young Black men sat down at a whites-only lunch counter and refused to leave. It was a simple act, but its message was deafening: segregation is unjust, and we won't stand for it any longer. That act sparked a wave of sit-ins across the country, galvanizing the civil rights movement.

The key here is simplicity. The sit-ins didn't require a manifesto or a megaphone. The deed itself carried the message, as clear and sharp as a slap to the face.

2. Strategic Timing

A deed is only as powerful as its timing. Even the boldest action can fall flat if it lands at the wrong moment, like a punchline delivered in an empty room. Successful deeds align with the rhythms of history, tapping into the energy of the moment and amplifying it.

Think of the storming of the Bastille in 1789. France was already a powder keg, simmering with anger over inequality and oppression. The Bastille wasn't just a fortress; it was a symbol of royal tyranny. When the revolutionaries took it, their action wasn't just dramatic—it was perfectly timed. It unleashed the fury of the people and became the defining moment of the French Revolution.

Timing isn't just about luck. It's about reading the room, sensing the cracks in the system, and striking when the iron is hot.

3. Broad Public Resonance

The most effective deeds aren't just about the activists—they're about everyone. They tap into shared fears, hopes, and frustrations, making the struggle feel personal to the wider public.

Consider Gandhi's Salt March in 1930. It wasn't just about salt; it was about the British Empire's stranglehold on India's resources and sovereignty. By focusing on something as universal as salt—a staple of daily life—Gandhi made the struggle relatable to millions.

This is the secret sauce of success: make your audience feel like they're part of the story.

The Roots of Failure

For every successful deed, there's a cautionary tale, a story of failure that serves as a warning. Sometimes, the deed is too extreme, alienating the very people it's meant to inspire. Other times, it fizzles out, forgotten before it has a chance to make an impact.

1. Lack of Clear Goals

One of the biggest pitfalls is acting without a clear purpose. If your deed is confusing or unfocused, it risks being dismissed as meaningless spectacle.

Take the 1999 WTO protests in Seattle. The movement brought thousands of activists to the streets, and their energy was undeniable. But the protests lacked a unified message, with groups advocating for everything from environmental justice to labor rights. The result? The media painted the protesters as chaotic and directionless, undermining their cause.

A deed without a clear goal is like a lighthouse with a broken bulb: it might draw attention, but it won't guide anyone to safety.

2. Alienating the Audience

Another common pitfall is alienation. When a deed is too radical or violent, it risks turning potential allies into critics.

Consider the Unabomber, Ted Kaczynski. His bombings were meant to draw attention to the dangers of industrial society, but his actions were so extreme that they overshadowed his message. Instead of sparking a meaningful conversation, he became a pariah, his ideas buried beneath the horror of his deeds.

The lesson here is balance. A deed must provoke without repelling, inspire without terrifying.

3. Misreading the Moment

Timing cuts both ways. Just as strategic timing can amplify a deed, poor timing can render it irrelevant or even counterproductive.

In 2011, a group of activists attempted to blockade the Keystone XL pipeline, hoping to draw attention to climate change. While their cause was just, their action was poorly timed. Public awareness of climate issues was still nascent, and the protest failed to gain widespread support.

Timing isn't just about seizing the moment; it's about creating a moment that people are ready to rally around.

Lessons from the Battlefield

Successes and failures aren't just stories—they're lessons. They teach us what works, what doesn't, and how to walk the fine line between inspiration and alienation.

1. The Power of Symbolism

Whether it's a sit-in, a march, or a protest, the most effective deeds are steeped in symbolism. They turn abstract ideas into tangible actions, giving people something to rally around.

Think of the Berlin Wall. When it fell in 1989, it wasn't just a physical barrier coming down—it was a symbol of the Cold War's end. The images of people tearing down the wall with their bare hands resonated across the globe, cementing the moment in history.

2. The Importance of Storytelling

A deed isn't just an action—it's a story. And like any good story, it needs heroes, villains, and a clear narrative arc.

Take the Black Panthers' armed patrols in the 1960s. They weren't just carrying guns; they were telling a story about self-defense, empowerment, and resistance. That story inspired countless others, transforming the Panthers into a symbol of Black liberation.

3. The Need for Follow-Through

A deed is just the beginning. Without follow-through, even the boldest action can fade into obscurity.

Consider the Montgomery Bus Boycott. Rosa Parks' arrest was the spark, but it was the sustained boycott—led by activists like Martin Luther King Jr.—that turned the spark into a roaring fire.

The Fine Line

Propaganda of the deed is a high-wire act, a balancing act between inspiration and alienation, success and failure. It's not a science—it's an art, one that requires intuition, strategy, and a deep understanding of the moment.

The difference between success and failure often comes down to intent. A deed rooted in justice, clarity, and purpose will resonate, even if it faces criticism or backlash. But a deed born of chaos, confusion, or ego will falter, leaving nothing but ashes in its wake.

So, learn from the past. Study the successes and failures, the triumphs and tragedies. And remember: the power of propaganda of the deed isn't in the act itself—it's in the ripples it creates, the stories it tells, and the movements it inspires.

Chapter 17: Defining Your Objectives

The thing about lighting a fire is that you have to know where you want the flames to go. A campfire warms you. A controlled burn clears the forest floor for new growth. A wildfire? Well, that's destruction for destruction's sake. Propaganda of the deed, as dramatic and fiery as it can be, isn't about burning everything down—it's about making a spark so bright and so perfectly aimed that it lights up the path forward.

But to do that, you need a target, an objective, a reason for people to sit up and take notice. And this isn't just about the big, showy act. It's about the why. Why are you doing this? Why does it matter? Why will it resonate? Without those answers, you're not lighting a fire—you're playing with matches in the wind.

Let's talk about defining your objectives. Not in a dry, strategic manual kind of way. Let's get into the guts of it, the heart of it, the part that makes this more than just some glorified stunt. This is where you find your purpose, your vision. This is where you make it matter.

Know Thyself (and Thy Cause)

Let's start with the basics: what are you fighting for? This sounds simple, but trust me, it's not. Plenty of people think they know what they're doing until someone asks them to explain it, and then their words twist and tangle like a phone cord in a teenager's bedroom.

So, step one: clarity. What's your cause? Not in a vague, "we want justice" kind of way, but in specifics. Is it worker's rights? Climate action? Racial justice? And within that, what exactly are you hoping to achieve?

Take the Civil Rights Movement in the United States. The leaders weren't just fighting for "equality" in some broad, hazy sense. They had specific objectives: ending segregation, securing voting rights, dismantling Jim Crow laws. These weren't just lofty ideals—they were concrete, actionable goals.

Your cause needs the same kind of specificity. You can't just say you're fighting the system. What part of the system? What do you want to dismantle, and what do you want to replace it with? If you don't know, no one else will either.

The Power of Focus

Once you've got your cause, you need to narrow it down. Think of it like a magnifying glass. A wide beam of light is harmless, but focus it just right, and you can set a leaf—or a whole movement—on fire.

Focus doesn't mean you're ignoring the bigger picture. It means you're choosing the part of the picture that will make the biggest impact right now.

Let's look at the Suffragettes. They wanted women's equality, a sweeping, transformative goal. But they focused their efforts on one specific objective: the right to vote. Why? Because it was achievable, it was tangible, and it was a stepping stone to everything else.

The same goes for you. What's the one thing you can tackle that will make the biggest difference? Maybe it's shutting down a polluting factory. Maybe it's overturning a discriminatory policy. Whatever it is, make it specific, make it clear, and make it something people can rally around.

Pick Your Battlefield

Objectives don't exist in a vacuum. They're tied to context, to place, to time. Where and when you act can be just as important as what you're acting for.

Think of the Stonewall Riots. The objective wasn't just to resist police brutality—it was to claim space, to say, "We belong here, and you can't push us out." Stonewall was a physical and symbolic battlefield, one that resonated with the LGBTQ+ community and beyond.

Your battlefield might not be a literal place. It could be a courtroom, a legislative chamber, or even the digital sphere. The key is to choose a space where your objective has the most impact, where it can't be ignored.

And timing? Timing is everything. Rosa Parks didn't just decide to sit on that bus seat one random afternoon. The Montgomery Bus Boycott had been brewing for months, and her act was the spark at just the right moment. Timing isn't just about luck—it's about preparation, about reading the currents of history and knowing when to strike.

Align with the Movement

Here's the thing: propaganda of the deed isn't a solo act. It's part of a symphony, a movement, a broader fight. Your objective needs to align with that fight, to amplify it rather than detract from it.

Take the Black Panthers' community programs. Their goal wasn't just to feed hungry kids or provide free medical care. It was to show the failures of the system, to prove that change was possible and necessary. Their deeds aligned with the broader fight for racial and economic justice, and that alignment made their actions even more powerful.

This isn't about playing second fiddle. It's about understanding that your action is one thread in a larger tapestry. The stronger your connection to the movement, the more powerful your action will be.

Make It Achievable

This is where a lot of people stumble. They set objectives so grand, so sprawling, that they're doomed to fail. And when they fail, the movement takes the hit.

Achievable doesn't mean small. It means realistic, within reach. It means setting a goal that's big enough to matter but focused enough to succeed.

Take the environmental activists who blocked Keystone XL. Their objective wasn't to dismantle the entire fossil fuel industry in one go. It was to stop one pipeline, one piece of the puzzle. That focus made their victory possible—and that victory inspired others.

Your objective should be a stretch, but not a leap into the void. It should challenge you without crushing you.

The Emotional Core

Let's get to the heart of it: why should people care? This is where the rubber meets the road, where your objective stops being just a goal and starts being a rallying cry.

Every great act of propaganda of the deed has an emotional core. It's not just about logic or strategy—it's about feeling, about tapping into the hopes, fears, and frustrations of the people you're trying to reach.

Think of Greta Thunberg's school strike for climate. Her objective was clear: to demand action on climate change. But what made her act so powerful was its emotional core. She wasn't just a teenager with a sign—she was a symbol of a generation fighting for its future. Her deed resonated because it spoke to something deeper than policy—it spoke to survival, to justice, to hope.

Your objective needs that kind of resonance. It needs to matter not just intellectually, but viscerally.

The Measure of Success

How will you know if you've succeeded? This might seem obvious, but it's not. Plenty of activists set objectives without ever defining what success looks like.

Success doesn't have to mean total victory. Sometimes it's about progress, about moving the needle. The Montgomery Bus Boycott didn't end racism, but it desegregated the buses. The sit-ins didn't dismantle segregation overnight, but they shifted public opinion.

Define your metrics. Maybe it's passing a law, sparking a conversation, or inspiring others to join the fight. Whatever it is, make it clear, make it measurable, and make it something you can build on.

The Fire That Burns Bright

Defining your objectives isn't just the first step—it's the foundation of everything. Without clear, focused, achievable goals, even the boldest action risks fading into the noise.

But with the right objectives, your deed becomes more than just an act. It becomes a spark, a flame, a fire that burns so bright it lights up the path forward.

So, take your time. Think it through. Define your purpose, your battlefield, your story. And then, when the moment comes, strike with all the power and clarity you can muster. Because when you do, you're not just acting—you're shaping history.

Chapter 18: Crafting Your Message

Actions might speak louder than words, but without the right message, even the loudest action can fade into a whisper. A deed on its own is just noise—what gives it power is the story it tells, the way it resonates with the people who see it. If propaganda of the deed is your flame, then the message is the oxygen. Without it, your spark sputters and dies.

So, let's talk about how to craft that message. Not just slap it together with duct tape and good intentions but really shape it, refine it, breathe life into it. Because if you want your action to land—really land—you can't leave the message to chance.

Message First, Action Second

Here's the thing: a lot of people get this backward. They think about the action first—the big dramatic thing they're going to do—and only afterward start scrambling to figure out what it all means. That's how you end up with confusing, self-indulgent stunts that might grab attention for a moment but leave everyone asking, "What the hell was that about?"

The best deeds, the ones that make history, always start with the message. Take the Boston Tea Party, for example. The Sons of Liberty didn't just decide to throw some tea in the harbor because it sounded fun. They had a clear message: *no taxation without representation.* The act itself was dramatic, sure, but what gave it power was the story it told about rebellion, freedom, and defiance.

So before you even think about what you're going to do, ask yourself: what are you trying to say? What's the story you want your action to tell?

The Three Questions

When crafting your message, there are three questions you need to answer. Think of them as the holy trinity of effective propaganda of the deed.

1. Who Are You Speaking To?

Your message isn't for everyone. In fact, if you try to speak to everyone, you'll probably end up speaking to no one. Effective deeds are targeted—they're aimed at a specific audience with a specific set of values, fears, and frustrations.

Think about Rosa Parks. When she refused to give up her seat, her message wasn't just for the racist establishment—it was for the Black community in Montgomery, a rallying cry to spark the bus boycott. Her action resonated because it was tailored to the people who needed to hear it most.

Who's your audience? Is it the workers on the factory floor? The students in the classroom? The policymakers in Washington? Whoever it is, make sure your message speaks directly to them, in language they understand and care about.

2. What Do You Want Them to Feel?

Propaganda of the deed is about more than facts and logic. It's about emotion. You're not just trying to make people think—you're trying to make them feel.

Do you want them to feel anger? Hope? Fear? Urgency? Look at Greta Thunberg. Her climate strikes aren't just about the science—they're about the raw, gut-wrenching fear of a stolen future. That's what makes her message hit so hard.

Emotion is the hook that draws people in, the spark that turns passive spectators into active participants. Find the emotion at the heart of your message, and lean into it.

3. What Do You Want Them to Do?

This is where a lot of activists drop the ball. They stage some big, dramatic action, get people's attention, and then...nothing. No call to action, no next step, no clear path forward.

Don't leave your audience hanging. If your deed is the spark, your call to action is the kindling. Tell people exactly what you want them to do, whether it's joining a protest, signing a petition, or simply paying attention. Make it clear, make it actionable, and make it something they can do right now.

Symbolism: The Heart of the Message

A good message isn't just clear—it's symbolic. It takes a complex issue and distills it into something simple, tangible, and unforgettable.

Take the Suffragettes smashing windows in London. They weren't just breaking glass—they were shattering the illusion that women would sit quietly and wait for their rights. The broken windows became a symbol of defiance, of the cracks forming in the patriarchal system.

Symbolism works because it's visceral. It bypasses logic and speaks directly to the heart. When crafting your message, think about what symbols you can use to amplify your story. A raised fist. A chained gate. A tree planted in defiance of a bulldozer. Symbols stick in people's minds long after the action is over.

Clarity: The Death of Ambiguity

The enemy of a good message is ambiguity. If people have to guess what your deed means, you've already lost. Your message needs to be so clear, so unmistakable, that even a distracted, half-asleep spectator can grasp it in an instant.

Think of Colin Kaepernick taking a knee during the national anthem. There was no ambiguity there. His action was a clear, powerful statement against police brutality and racial injustice. The simplicity of it—the quiet, deliberate nature of the gesture—made it impossible to ignore.

When planning your deed, strip away anything that muddies the waters. Focus on what matters, and make it impossible to misunderstand.

Matching the Deed to the Message

Your action and your message are a package deal. One without the other is like a bird with a broken wing—it's not going anywhere.

The best deeds don't just align with their message—they embody it. Gandhi's Salt March wasn't just about opposing British rule; it was about reclaiming India's resources and autonomy. By marching to the sea and making salt, Gandhi turned his message into a physical, tangible act.

Ask yourself: does your action reflect your message? Does it reinforce the story you're trying to tell? If not, rethink it. The deed should be the living, breathing embodiment of your message.

The Role of Media

In today's world, your audience isn't just the people who witness your action firsthand—it's the millions who see it through the media. Whether it's a viral video, a headline, or a tweet, the media is how your message travels.

But here's the catch: the media loves to twist, distort, and sensationalize. If you're not careful, your deed can be misrepresented, your message lost in the noise.

To counter this, you need to be proactive. Have spokespeople ready to explain your action. Craft a press release that lays out your message clearly and concisely. Use social media to tell your story in your own words.

And remember: the visuals matter. A powerful image can spread faster than a thousand words, so think about how your action will look on camera.

Anticipating the Backlash

No matter how clear and powerful your message is, there will always be people who try to twist it, discredit it, or drown it out. That's the nature of the game.

The key is to anticipate the backlash and prepare for it. What criticisms are you likely to face? How can you counter them? The more prepared you are, the harder it will be for your opponents to derail your message.

And don't forget: sometimes backlash can work in your favor. When the media demonized the Black Panthers, it only highlighted the failures of the system they were fighting against. Use the backlash to reinforce your story, not undermine it.

The Long Tail of the Message

A deed is a moment, but a message can last a lifetime. The most effective deeds aren't just about the immediate impact—they're about planting seeds that will grow long after the action is over.

Think of the Occupy Wall Street movement. The encampments are gone, but the message—the idea of the 99% vs. the 1%—is still part of our cultural vocabulary. That's the power of a good message: it sticks, it spreads, and it keeps on resonating.

When crafting your message, think about the long game. What do you want people to remember? What story do you want to linger in their minds?

Speak Loud, Speak True

Crafting your message isn't just about words. It's about clarity, emotion, and resonance. It's about creating something so powerful, so unforgettable, that it echoes long after the deed is done.

So, take your time. Get it right. Think about your audience, your symbols, your story. And when the moment comes, speak loud, speak true, and let your message blaze like a signal fire in the night. Because if you do it right, people won't just see your action—they'll feel it, remember it, and carry it forward.

Chapter 19: Nonviolent vs. Violent Action

It's a fork in the road that every movement, every revolutionary, every would-be catalyst for change must face sooner or later. To fight without raising a fist or to fight with blood in your eyes? That's the question. Nonviolence and violence are two sides of a very old coin, and neither is as straightforward as its champions—or detractors—might have you believe.

And here's the thing: the road you choose shapes everything. It's not just about tactics. It's about morality, public perception, legacy. It's about what story you want the world to tell when your deed becomes history.

But let's not get ahead of ourselves. Let's pull up a chair, light a candle, and take a long, hard look at these two paths, their pros, their cons, and the ghosts of those who've walked them before.

The Case for Nonviolence: The Quiet Power of Peace

Nonviolence, on the surface, sounds like the easy choice. It's palatable, noble, the high road. But don't mistake it for weakness. Nonviolence is a blade that cuts sharp and deep—if you know how to wield it.

Take Gandhi. He didn't need bullets to bring the British Empire to its knees. He used salt, spinning wheels, and hunger strikes. Simple, symbolic acts that carried the weight of a billion voices. Or Martin Luther King Jr., whose marches and sit-ins painted a picture of dignity and courage in the face of fire hoses and police dogs.

Nonviolence works because it's disarming. It forces your enemy into a corner, exposing their brutality while you stand firm and resolute. It's hard to paint someone as a villain when they're marching with flowers in their hands and songs on their lips.

Pros of Nonviolent Action

1. **Moral High Ground**: Nonviolence gives you the moral edge. It's a tough sell to demonize a movement that refuses to harm anyone, no matter how righteous their anger might be.
2. **Public Sympathy**: Images of peaceful protesters being beaten or arrested hit hard. They stir something deep in people, a primal sense of right and wrong.
3. **Inclusivity**: Nonviolent movements often attract a broader base. Parents, students, elders—people who might shy away from violent conflict feel safer standing behind a peaceful cause.
4. **Longevity**: Nonviolence builds movements that endure. You're not just fighting for a moment—you're laying the groundwork for a better future.

Cons of Nonviolent Action

But let's not romanticize it. Nonviolence has its pitfalls, too.

1. **Slow Progress**: Change through nonviolence is often glacial. It takes years, decades even, to see results. And in the meantime, people are still suffering.
2. **Limited by Opponents' Conscience**: Nonviolence relies on your adversaries having a shred of humanity. Against a truly ruthless enemy, it can feel like shouting into the void.
3. **Vulnerability**: Peaceful protesters are sitting ducks. They're exposed, unarmed, at the mercy of police batons and angry mobs.
4. **Requires Patience and Unity**: Nonviolence demands discipline and restraint. All it takes is one hothead throwing a punch to derail the whole movement.

The Case for Violence: The Fire of Revolt

Now, let's step into the shadows for a moment. Let's talk about violence—not as an abstract idea, but as a tool, a weapon, a necessary evil.

Because sometimes, the world doesn't listen to flowers and marches. Sometimes, the oppressor doesn't flinch at hunger strikes or petitions. Sometimes, the only language they understand is fire.

Frantz Fanon didn't shy away from this truth. In *The Wretched of the Earth*, he argued that violence isn't just a tool for the colonized—it's a cleansing force, a way to reclaim dignity and humanity. And then there's Malcolm X, who reminded us that if someone lays a hand on you, you send them to the cemetery.

Violence shocks the system. It disrupts, destabilizes, and demands attention. It's messy, dangerous, and unpredictable. But it's also powerful, and sometimes, it's the only way to break the chains.

Pros of Violent Action

1. **Immediate Impact**: Violence gets results—fast. It forces people to pay attention, to act, to respond.
2. **Deterrence**: A violent uprising sends a clear message: we won't be pushed around anymore. It makes the oppressor think twice before cracking the whip again.
3. **Empowerment**: For the oppressed, taking up arms can be a way to reclaim power, to feel like they're not just victims anymore.
4. **Systemic Disruption**: Violence can topple regimes, dismantle institutions, and create the kind of chaos that leads to change.

Cons of Violent Action

But violence comes with a heavy price. It's a double-edged sword that can just as easily cut you down.

1. **Public Backlash**: Violence alienates people. It's hard to win hearts and minds when you're burning buildings and shedding blood.
2. **Escalation**: Violence breeds violence. What starts as a justified uprising can spiral into a cycle of retaliation, leaving devastation in its wake.
3. **Moral Compromise**: The line between justified

violence and senseless brutality is razor-thin. Cross it, and you risk losing your soul—and your cause.

4. **Unpredictable Outcomes**: Violence is chaos. Once you unleash it, you can't control where it goes or what it leaves behind.

When to Choose Nonviolence

So, how do you decide? When is nonviolence the right path?

Nonviolence works best when you're fighting a system that still has a conscience, however faint. Democracies, for all their flaws, are fertile ground for nonviolent resistance. They rely on public opinion, on the illusion of fairness and justice.

It's also effective when your goal is to build a broad-based movement. Nonviolence unites, inspires, and creates a sense of shared purpose. It's not just about defeating the enemy—it's about winning over the hearts and minds of the people.

When to Choose Violence

And violence? Violence is the path you take when there's no other choice. When the system is so corrupt, so brutal, that no amount of peaceful protest will make a dent.

Colonial regimes, military dictatorships, oppressive empires—these are the battlegrounds where violence becomes not just justified, but necessary. It's the last resort, the desperate cry of a people with nothing left to lose.

But even then, violence must be strategic, controlled. It's not about rage or revenge—it's about sending a message, forcing change, and knowing when to put the weapons down.

Blurring the Lines

Here's where it gets complicated: the line between nonviolence and violence isn't always clear. Take Nelson Mandela. He started as a peaceful activist, but when the apartheid regime refused to budge, he turned to sabotage. Was he a nonviolent leader? A revolutionary? Both?

Movements often shift between the two paths, adapting to the circumstances, the stakes, the enemy. And sometimes, the most effective strategy is to walk the razor's edge, combining peaceful protest with the threat of force.

The Ripple Effect

Whether you choose nonviolence or violence, remember this: your actions have ripples. They don't just affect your immediate cause—they shape the world's perception of your movement, your people, your legacy.

Nonviolence creates a legacy of hope, dignity, and moral clarity. But it can also leave you vulnerable, your sacrifices forgotten if the change doesn't come fast enough.

Violence carves a path of fear and power. It gets results, but it leaves scars—on your enemies, on your people, on your soul.

The Choice Is Yours

There's no easy answer, no universal truth. Nonviolence and violence are tools, and like any tool, their effectiveness depends on how and when you use them.

So ask yourself: What are you fighting for? Who are you fighting against? What story do you want the world to tell about you when the dust settles?

And then choose. Choose wisely. Because once you take that first step—whether it's with a flower in your hand or a Molotov cocktail—you can't go back.

Chapter 20: Building a Team

You can't do it alone. Sure, lone wolves make for great legends—Robin Hood with his merry band, the grim assassin slipping through the shadows, the rebel with a cause and a dynamite stick in his hand—but that's just the surface of the story. Behind every lone wolf is a pack, even if it's hidden in the trees, howling at the moon.

Building a team isn't just about numbers. It's about trust, cohesion, and shared vision. It's about knowing who's got your back when the night gets dark and the stakes get higher than you ever imagined. It's about assembling a group of people who aren't just willing to fight for the cause but will hold steady when the world tries to pull them apart.

So, let's talk about the how, the why, and the who. Pull up a chair, grab a cup of coffee—or something stronger—and let's get to work.

Why a Team Matters

You might be thinking, "I've got passion, I've got drive—why do I need anyone else?" And for a little while, maybe you don't. Maybe you can storm the gates, plant the seeds, light the first spark all on your own.

But here's the thing: a revolution isn't a solo act. It's a symphony. You can't conduct an orchestra with one violin, no matter how well you play it.

A team brings strength in numbers, sure, but it also brings diversity of thought, skill, and experience. You're not a jack-of-all-trades, no matter how much you want to be. A good team fills in the gaps, covers your blind spots, and makes sure the foundation doesn't crumble when the weight of the world comes crashing down.

Step 1: Define the Vision

Before you start looking for people, you need to know what you're building. A team without a clear purpose is just a group of people waiting for something to happen.

What's your mission? Is it to disrupt, inspire, create? Are you looking to tear down a system or build a new one? What are your non-negotiables, your red lines? Write it down, scream it from the rooftops if you must. But make sure it's clear, compelling, and concrete.

People follow clarity. They rally around ideas that feel bigger than themselves. If your vision is foggy, your team will scatter the moment things get tough.

Step 2: Find Your Core

You don't start with a crowd; you start with a spark. The core team is the heart of the movement—the people who'll stay when everyone else runs, who'll fight when it feels like the fight is lost.

Look for people who share your vision, but don't just settle for nodding heads. Challenge them, let them challenge you. The best teammates aren't the ones who agree with you all the time;

they're the ones who make your ideas sharper, your strategies stronger.

Qualities to Look For

- **Commitment**: Are they in it for the long haul, or are they just chasing a momentary thrill?

- **Integrity**: Can you trust them with your plans, your secrets, your life?

- **Skill**: What can they do that you can't? What do they bring to the table?

- **Adaptability**: Can they think on their feet, roll with the punches, and stay steady when the ground shifts beneath them?

Step 3: Build Trust, Brick by Brick

Trust is the glue that holds a team together, and it doesn't come cheap. It's earned, piece by piece, through shared experience, vulnerability, and time.

Practical Tips for Building Trust

1. **Start Small**: Don't jump into the deep end right away. Test the waters with small projects, low-stakes missions. See how people handle pressure, responsibility, and failure.
2. **Be Transparent**: Secrets are poison to a team. Share your vision, your plans, your fears. Let people know

where you're coming from and where you're trying to go.

3. **Own Your Mistakes**: When you screw up—and you will—own it. Nothing destroys trust faster than a leader who can't admit when they're wrong.

4. **Create Space for Connection**: Teams aren't built in meetings or strategy sessions. They're built in the in-between moments—over meals, late-night conversations, shared laughter.

Step 4: Organize Without Suffocating

Here's the tricky part: you need structure, but not too much. A rigid hierarchy might keep things orderly, but it kills creativity, adaptability, and ownership. On the other hand, total anarchy leads to chaos and infighting.

Key Roles to Consider

- **The Strategist**: The big-picture thinker who maps out the road ahead.

- **The Organizer**: The detail-oriented planner who keeps the wheels turning.

- **The Communicator**: The voice of the team, crafting messages that resonate.

- **The Specialist**: The person with the technical skills, whether it's hacking, design, logistics, or anything else.

- **The Fixer:** The one who knows how to solve problems, navigate conflict, and keep everyone grounded.

But don't pigeonhole people. Roles should be fluid, allowing team members to step up or step back as needed.

Step 5: Handle Conflict Head-On

Conflict is inevitable. You're bringing together passionate, driven people with strong opinions and big ideas. Sparks will fly, and sometimes those sparks will ignite fires.

The key is to address conflict early, openly, and with respect. Let it simmer too long, and it'll explode. Try to suppress it, and it'll fester.

Conflict Resolution Tips

1. **Listen First:** Before jumping to conclusions, hear people out. Let them vent, express their frustrations, and feel heard.
2. **Focus on Solutions:** Don't get bogged down in blame. Shift the conversation toward what can be done to move forward.
3. **Set Boundaries:** Healthy teams need clear boundaries—what's acceptable, what's not, and what happens when someone crosses the line.
4. **Know When to Let Go:** Sometimes, despite your best efforts, a team member just doesn't fit. Don't drag it out. Part ways respectfully but decisively.

Step 6: Keep the Flame Alive

Movements fade when the fire dies out. Even the most passionate team can burn out, lose focus, or drift apart if the spark isn't nurtured.

Ways to Maintain Momentum

- **Celebrate Wins**: Big or small, every victory matters. Celebrate them. Let your team see the fruits of their labor.

- **Revisit the Vision**: Remind people why they started, what they're fighting for, and what's at stake.

- **Foster Growth**: Encourage learning, skill development, and personal growth. A stagnant team is a dying team.

- **Stay Connected**: Regular check-ins, retreats, or even casual hangouts can keep the bonds strong.

The Power of Cohesion

A team isn't just a collection of individuals—it's a living, breathing organism. It moves as one, thinks as one, fights as one. And when it works, when all the pieces click into place, it's unstoppable.

So build your team like your life depends on it—because someday, it might. Choose your people carefully, nurture them fiercely, and never take them for granted.

Because when the storm comes—and it will—you're going to need them. All of them.

Chapter 21: Legal and Ethical Considerations

No one sets out to change the world without picking a fight. Sometimes it's with a corrupt system, a stubborn status quo, or a society too comfortable in its apathy. But every fight has rules—or at least consequences—and navigating those waters without sinking is a fine art.

Picture yourself standing on a tightrope, high above a chasm. On one side: legality. On the other: morality. Below you: consequences that don't care about your intentions. That's what this chapter is about—walking that line, balancing the risks, and making damn sure you can look yourself in the mirror when it's all said and done.

What's the Risk? Understanding Legal Frameworks

You're not a kid anymore; ignorance isn't an excuse. If you're diving into the realm of propaganda of the deed, you need to know the legal ramifications. Law enforcement, courts, and governments aren't just abstract systems—they're engines that grind up people who don't understand the rules.

The first question you have to ask yourself is simple: how far are you willing to go? Because once you cross certain lines, there's no coming back.

Know the Laws, Break Them Intelligently

- **Research Your Jurisdiction**: Every country, state, or province has its own legal codes. What's considered free speech in one place might be criminalized in another.

- **Understand the Grey Areas**: Some actions aren't explicitly illegal but can still get you into hot water—trespassing, obstruction, or even failure to comply with law enforcement.

- **Lawyers Are Your Friends**: You don't need to have one on speed dial (although that helps), but you should at least consult one during your planning phase. Understand what's at stake before you act.

The Risks of Not Knowing

Let's say you pull off a dramatic protest—chaining yourself to a corporate office door, for instance. You think you're making a bold statement. Then the cops show up, and suddenly you're looking at charges for vandalism, trespassing, and incitement. What you thought was a slap on the wrist turns into something that could ruin your life.

The bottom line? Ignorance can be a weapon against you. Don't hand it over willingly.

Staying Ethical in a Messy World

It's not just about what's legal—it's about what's right. This is where things get murky. Morality doesn't live in black and white; it thrives in shades of grey. What's ethical to you might be despicable to someone else. The key is to define your own moral boundaries and stick to them, even when the heat is on.

The Question of Violence

Let's address the elephant in the room. Is violence ever justified? For some, the answer is a hard no. For others, it's a calculated decision—a last resort when every peaceful avenue has been exhausted. The author of this book does not condone violence.

Consider these:

- **Collateral Damage**: Who else is going to get hurt, intentionally or not? The more innocent casualties there are, the harder it is to defend your actions.

- **Long-Term Effects**: Will your deed inspire others to rise up, or will it make your cause look dangerous and unstable?

History is full of examples on both sides of the spectrum. Gandhi and Martin Luther King Jr. wielded nonviolence like a scalpel, while groups like the Weather Underground opted for bombs. Both strategies had their successes and failures. The difference is how history remembers them—and how their actions shaped the world.

Integrity Over Everything

You're going to face temptations. Shortcuts. Moments where it would be so much easier to compromise your principles for the sake of the mission. Don't do it. The second you lose sight of your values, you've lost everything.

Keep this in mind:

- **Transparency**: Lies will always come back to bite you. Be honest with your team, your allies, and yourself.

- **Accountability**: If you make a mistake, own it. Don't pass the blame or try to cover it up.

- **The Big Picture**: Ask yourself if your actions align with your ultimate goals. If they don't, walk away.

Protecting Yourself and Your Team

Let's talk self-preservation. You can't change the world from a jail cell—or worse, a morgue. Staying safe, both legally and physically, is a crucial part of the game.

Legal Precautions

1. **Document Everything**: Keep records of your plans, communications, and any evidence that supports the legality of your actions. If something goes sideways, you'll need it.
2. **Don't Act Alone**: A lone individual is an easy target. A coordinated team can share the load and provide alibis if needed.
3. **Know Your Rights**: Familiarize yourself with your

rights in public spaces, during protests, or if you're detained. Knowledge is power.

Physical Precautions

1. **Disguise and Deception**: Surveillance is everywhere. Masks, hats, and nondescript clothing can protect your identity during actions.
2. **Escape Routes**: Always have an exit strategy. Know the area, and have multiple ways to get out quickly if things go south.
3. **Emergency Contacts**: Make sure someone outside your immediate team knows where you are and what you're doing.

The Digital Battlefield

We live in an age where your phone is both a tool and a liability. Every message, search, and GPS ping leaves a trail that authorities can—and will—follow.

How to Stay Safe Online

- **Use Encryption**: Apps like Signal and ProtonMail offer end-to-end encryption, making it harder for third parties to access your communications.

- **Stay Anonymous**: Use VPNs, Tor browsers, and burner accounts to mask your digital footprint.

- **Avoid Oversharing**: Social media is not your friend. Posting details about your plans, locations, or team members is like handing law enforcement a roadmap to your doorstep. Remember, Ted Kaczynski would have been the last person to have an online presence and he was caught because his manifesto contained a turn of phrase he was known to use, "You can't eat your cake and have it too" instead of the usual "You can't have your cake and eat it too."

The Balance Between Fear and Freedom

Here's the hardest part. The more risks you take, the more cautious you have to be. But caution can easily slide into paranoia, and paranoia can paralyze you. The goal is to stay vigilant without losing your nerve.

How to Manage Fear

- **Focus on the Mission**: Fear is a reaction; courage is a decision. Keep your eyes on the prize, and let that guide you.

- **Rely on Your Team**: Trust the people around you. If you've chosen well, they'll help keep you grounded.

- **Practice Resilience**: Prepare for setbacks, legal troubles, and public backlash. The stronger your resolve, the harder it'll be for outside forces to shake you.

When the Hammer Falls

Let's say the worst happens. You're caught, charged, and facing the full weight of the legal system. What now?

Stay Calm, Stay Quiet

- **Invoke Your Rights**: You have the right to remain silent and the right to an attorney. Use them.

- **Don't Incriminate Yourself**: Anything you say can and will be used against you. Be polite but firm—no statements without legal counsel.

Leverage the Public Eye

Sometimes, being caught can amplify your cause. Trials can turn into platforms, martyrs into movements. Think about how the Chicago Seven or Nelson Mandela used their arrests to shine a spotlight on injustice.

But remember: that only works if your actions align with your principles. If you've strayed, the spotlight will expose your flaws, not your cause.

Staying True to Yourself

When the dust settles and you're alone with your thoughts, the only thing that matters is whether you stayed true to yourself. Legal and ethical considerations aren't just external—they're internal, too.

Did you act with integrity? Did you inspire change, or did you sow chaos? Were you brave, or were you reckless? These are the questions you'll have to answer, not just for the world, but for yourself.

So take a deep breath, steady your hands, and make your move. But whatever you do, don't forget to look in the mirror before you act—and make sure you like the person staring back at you.

Chapter 22: The Role of Media

When the deed is done, when the dust settles and the crowd has dispersed, what's left? Is it just the adrenaline, the satisfied thrum of your heartbeat reminding you that you pulled it off? Or is there something bigger—a ripple spreading out, touching corners of the world you've never been to, faces you'll never see?

That ripple is media.

In the digital age, where a single tweet can spark a revolution or bury one, the role of media isn't just important—it's everything. Without eyes on your action, without words to carry the meaning, without images to capture the moment, your deed is a tree falling in the forest with no one around to hear it.

The media isn't just a tool for amplifying your message—it's a battlefield. And if you want to win, you'd better know how to fight on it.

The Two-Faced Beast: Traditional and Social Media

Before we dive into the nitty-gritty, let's get one thing straight: "the media" isn't a monolith. It's a two-faced beast, split between the old guard of traditional media—newspapers, TV news, radio—and the chaotic, wild west of social media.

Traditional Media

The newspapers and TV stations are the heavy hitters. They've got the reach, the reputation, and the resources to put your deed in front of millions. But they're also gatekeepers. They'll filter your message, slap their own spin on it, and decide whether you're a hero, a villain, or just another footnote in the evening news.

Social Media

Social media is where the rules get thrown out the window. Anyone can post, share, and comment. Virality is the golden ticket, but it's a fickle one—what resonates today can disappear tomorrow, buried under a flood of cat videos and outrage over the latest celebrity scandal.

Both types of media have their strengths and weaknesses, and if you want your deed to break through the noise, you've got to know how to play both sides.

Planning for Maximum Impact

A well-executed deed is like a well-written book—it's not just about what happens, but how the story is told. The media is your narrator, and if you want your story to be heard, you've got to plan every detail.

Step 1: Define Your Message

Before you even lift a finger, you need to know exactly what you want to say. Is your deed a cry for justice? A call to arms? A symbol of resistance? Whatever it is, boil it down to a single, clear message.

Ask yourself:

- What do I want people to feel when they hear about this?

- What action do I want them to take?

- How can I make my message impossible to ignore?

Step 2: Craft Your Visuals

Images are powerful. Think of the lone man standing in front of the tank in Tiananmen Square, or the burning effigies of colonial rulers during independence movements. A single image can encapsulate your entire message and burn it into the minds of millions.

Tips for crafting visuals:

- **Keep it Simple**: Complexity can dilute your message. Focus on bold, clear imagery.

- **Make it Memorable**: Use symbols, colors, or actions that stick in people's minds.

- **Think of the Angle**: Photographers and videographers will frame your deed in a certain way. Plan for it.

Step 3: Timing is Everything

PROPAGANDA OF THE DEED

The world runs on a 24-hour news cycle, and if you want to dominate it, you've got to pick your moment. Timing your deed to coincide with significant dates, anniversaries, or current events can make the difference between being front-page news and being buried in the back pages.

Working with Traditional Media

The old-school media may feel like dinosaurs compared to the frenetic pace of social platforms, but don't underestimate their power. A well-placed story in a reputable outlet can give your deed a level of legitimacy and reach that's hard to achieve otherwise.

Building Relationships with Journalists

Journalists aren't your enemies. They're storytellers, and they're always on the hunt for a good story. Make it easy for them:

- **Send a Press Release**: Keep it professional, concise, and packed with all the key details—who, what, where, when, and why.

- **Offer Access**: If it's safe and feasible, invite journalists to witness your deed firsthand.

- **Have a Spokesperson**: Designate someone to speak on behalf of your team. They should be articulate, knowledgeable, and prepared for tough questions.

Control the Narrative

Here's the catch: journalists will add their own interpretation to your deed. To minimize the risk of being misunderstood, anticipate their questions and have answers ready. Stick to your message, and don't let them twist your words.

Harnessing the Power of Social Media

If traditional media is a sniper rifle, social media is a shotgun. It's messy, unpredictable, and incredibly effective when used right.

Go Viral or Go Home

Virality isn't an exact science, but there are ways to tip the odds in your favor:

- **Create Shareable Content**: Videos, memes, and infographics are more likely to spread than long-winded statements.

- **Use Hashtags**: Jump on trending topics or create your own hashtag to consolidate the conversation.

- **Engage with Followers**: Respond to comments, answer questions, and keep the momentum going.

The Double-Edged Sword of Live Streaming

Live streaming can be a game-changer, giving people an unfiltered look at your deed as it unfolds. But it's a double-edged sword. Mistakes, missteps, or unforeseen complications will be broadcast in real-time. Make sure you're prepared for anything.

Dealing with Backlash

For every person who applauds your deed, there will be another who condemns it. Critics will come at you from all sides—opponents, skeptics, even supposed allies who think you've gone too far or not far enough.

Anticipate the Criticism

Before you act, think about how your deed might be received. Are there aspects that could be misunderstood? Weak points that critics might exploit? Address these issues in advance, and be ready to defend your actions.

Own the Narrative

The worst thing you can do is go silent. Engage with your critics, correct misinformation, and reinforce your message. If you don't control the narrative, someone else will—and you might not like what they say.

The Power of Persistence

A single deed might not change the world, but a series of deeds—each amplified through the media—can build unstoppable momentum. Think of it as a drumbeat, each action echoing louder and louder until the message becomes impossible to ignore.

The Long Game

The media loves novelty, but movements are built on consistency. Keep the story alive by following up with new actions, fresh angles, and updates on your progress.

Case Studies: Media and the Deed

Let's look at two examples of propaganda of the deed that mastered the media game:

1. **The Civil Rights Movement**: Images of police brutality against peaceful protesters—broadcast on national television—shocked the conscience of America and galvanized support for civil rights legislation.
2. **Extinction Rebellion**: By using theatrical stunts and social media-savvy tactics, Extinction Rebellion has kept the climate crisis in the headlines and mobilized millions worldwide.

Both movements understood the power of media and used it to their advantage. You can do the same.

Final Thoughts

At its core, propaganda of the deed is a conversation—one that starts with an action and echoes through the media. It's not enough to simply do something bold; you have to make sure the world is watching, listening, and understanding.

So plan your story, pick your moment, and seize the narrative. The world is your audience. Make it count.

Chapter 23: Logistics and Planning

They say that the devil's in the details, and when it comes to pulling off a deed that will resonate across the world—be it through awe, fear, or admiration—that devil sits front and center. You've got your vision, your message, your team. But without logistics, without the bones and sinew that hold it all together, you're just shouting into the void.

A well-planned action is like a symphony, every note in perfect harmony, every instrument tuned and ready. But a poorly planned one? That's a mess, a cacophony where the violins screech, the drums stumble, and the conductor throws up their hands in despair.

So, before you charge into the world with fire in your belly, let's talk about how to make sure your action doesn't just make a splash—it makes waves.

The Art of Preparation

The first step in executing any deed is understanding that spontaneity is a myth. Sure, the world loves a good story about a "spur-of-the-moment" protest or an "unplanned" act of resistance, but the truth is that the most impactful actions are meticulously planned down to the last detail.

Start with the Why

Everything begins with intent. Why are you doing this? What's the endgame? Maybe you want to disrupt, to inspire, to provoke. Maybe you're just trying to shine a spotlight on something the world would rather ignore. Whatever it is, write it down. Let it sit in your bones. Because when the going gets tough—and it will—you'll need to hold onto that "why" like a lifeline.

Scouting the Stage

Every deed needs a stage, a place where the drama unfolds and the world takes notice. But picking that stage isn't as simple as pointing to a map.

Location, Location, Location

Your location should be as much a part of the message as the action itself. Think about it: a protest on a quiet street might disrupt a handful of people, but a protest in front of a corporate headquarters or a government building? That's a headline waiting to happen.

When scouting your location, ask yourself:

- Does this place amplify my message?

- Is it symbolic of the issue I'm addressing?

- Will it attract the right audience or media attention?

The Lay of the Land

Once you've picked your spot, it's time to get familiar with it—intimately familiar. Walk the area. Note the entrances, exits, security cameras, and blind spots. Pay attention to patterns: when are the crowds thickest? When are they thinnest? When does the sun hit just right for that perfect photo op?

And always, always have an escape route.

Securing Resources

An idea without resources is like a car without fuel—it's not going anywhere.

The Essentials

Every action requires three things: people, tools, and money. Let's break it down.

1. **People**
   Your team is your most valuable resource, and they're more than just bodies in a crowd. You'll need organizers, communicators, lookouts, and maybe even a medic or two, depending on the risk level.

2. **Tools**
   Think of tools in broad terms: banners and megaphones, yes, but also bolt cutters, drones, or even just a sturdy pair of walking shoes. The tools you need depend entirely on the action you're planning, so make a list early and double-check it often.

3. **Money**
   Actions cost money, whether it's for transportation,

supplies, or legal fees if things go south. Fundraising is its own beast, but don't underestimate the power of community support. Crowdfunding platforms, benefit events, or even passing the hat at meetings can go a long way.

Contingencies

Murphy's Law states that anything that can go wrong, will go wrong. And when it does, you'll thank yourself for having a Plan B. Stockpile extra supplies, assign backup roles, and make sure everyone knows what to do if things don't go according to script.

Timing is Everything

The right action at the wrong time is the same as no action at all. Timing can make or break your deed, so don't leave it to chance.

When to Strike

Think about your audience. Are they more likely to pay attention during the morning rush hour, or in the dead of night? Is there a specific date or anniversary that ties into your message? Timing your deed to coincide with broader events can amplify its impact.

Pacing the Action

Some deeds are quick and explosive—light the match, set the fire, and disappear before anyone knows what hit them. Others are slow burns, designed to draw attention over hours or even days. Decide which approach fits your message, and plan accordingly.

Role Assignments

A successful action is like a heist movie: everyone has a role, and everyone knows it inside and out.

The Planner

That's you, or maybe someone else in your group. The planner sees the big picture, connects the dots, and keeps the whole operation running smoothly.

The Spokesperson

If media is expected, you'll need someone who can speak on behalf of the group. They should be articulate, confident, and unshakable under pressure.

The Lookouts

Every action needs eyes on the ground. Lookouts monitor for security, unexpected obstacles, or any signs of trouble.

The Doers

These are the people who execute the deed itself. They're the ones holding the banner, chaining themselves to the gate, or climbing the scaffolding. Make sure they're trained, equipped, and ready for anything.

The Documenters

If your action isn't captured, did it even happen? Assign someone to take photos, shoot video, and post updates to social media in real-time.

Risk Assessment and Mitigation

Every deed carries risks, and understanding those risks is crucial.

Physical Risks

Think about the safety of your team. Are there hazards at the location? Could your action provoke a violent response? Make sure everyone knows what they're getting into and how to protect themselves.

Legal Risks

Some actions skirt the line of legality, while others blow past it entirely. Research local laws, and have a plan in place for dealing with arrests. It's not a bad idea to have a lawyer on speed dial.

Emotional Risks

Deeds can be draining, both physically and emotionally. Debrief with your team afterward, and make space for people to process their experiences.

The Power of Practice

No matter how well you plan, there's no substitute for rehearsal. Run through your action step by step, and troubleshoot any issues that arise. Practice doesn't just smooth out the kinks—it builds confidence.

Case Studies: Logistics in Action

The Stonewall Riots

The Stonewall Riots weren't planned in the traditional sense, but their success came from quick thinking and adaptability. When the police raided the Stonewall Inn, the patrons didn't scatter—they regrouped, improvised, and turned the moment into a movement.

The Occupy Movement

Occupy Wall Street's success lay in its meticulous logistics. From setting up encampments to organizing food, medical care, and media outreach, the movement showed that planning isn't just about the deed—it's about sustaining it.

Final Thoughts

Logistics might not be glamorous, but it's the backbone of every great deed. Without it, even the most passionate actions can fall flat. So plan, rehearse, and prepare for the unexpected.

Because when the moment comes, when the world is watching, you'll want every detail to shine. And that's when the magic happens.

Chapter 24: Dealing with Backlash

Let's not kid ourselves—when you throw a rock at the hornet's nest, you're gonna get stung. Backlash is inevitable. If you're taking a stand, shaking up the status quo, or calling out some big, ugly truth, you can bet your last dollar that someone, somewhere, won't take it sitting down. And it won't just be your enemies sharpening their knives. Sometimes, it'll be the people you thought were on your side.

Here's the good news, though: backlash is a sign you've struck a nerve. The louder the howl, the deeper you've driven the nail. But surviving that backlash, and making sure your deed doesn't drown in the flood of criticism, takes more than just a thick skin. It takes strategy, resilience, and—when all else fails—a little bit of grit.

So, buckle up. This chapter is about navigating the storm you've stirred, and maybe even using it to your advantage.

Understanding the Nature of Backlash

Before we dive into how to deal with it, let's talk about what backlash actually is. It's more than just criticism or disapproval—it's a reaction to perceived threat. When people feel their power, beliefs, or way of life being challenged, they push back. Hard.

Backlash comes in different flavors, from public outrage to private whispers, and you need to be ready for all of it.

The Outrage Machine

Public backlash is the most visible and, often, the most overwhelming. Think headlines screaming your name, social media feeds flooded with vitriol, and talking heads debating your actions on the nightly news.

Institutional Pushback

This is the kind of backlash that comes from the powers that be. It might be legal action, new regulations, or even quiet retaliation like losing a job or being blacklisted.

Friendly Fire

This one stings the most: criticism from your allies. Maybe they think you've gone too far, or not far enough. Maybe they're just scared of being associated with your actions. Whatever the reason, it hurts—but it's something you have to prepare for.

Responding to Criticism

When the criticism starts pouring in, your instinct might be to fight back, to shout louder, to defend yourself at all costs. But knee-jerk reactions can do more harm than good. Instead, take a step back, breathe, and approach it with a clear head.

Listen and Learn

Not all criticism is bad. Sometimes, it's a chance to learn and grow. Ask yourself:

- Is the criticism valid?

- Does it come from a place of genuine concern?

- Can it help me improve my approach in the future?

If the answer is yes, don't be afraid to admit it. A little humility can go a long way.

Control the Narrative

In the age of social media, controlling the narrative is half the battle. If you let others define your action, you'll always be playing defense. So, take the initiative. Craft your own message, and make sure it's clear, compelling, and consistent.

Pick Your Battles

Not every critic deserves a response. Some people just want to stir the pot, and engaging with them only gives them more power. Know when to engage, when to ignore, and when to walk away.

Handling Legal Repercussions

If your deed skirts the edges of legality—or barrels straight through them—you need to be prepared for the fallout. Legal repercussions can range from fines and lawsuits to arrests and jail time.

Know Your Rights

Before you take action, make sure you understand the laws in your area. What's legal? What's not? What are the potential penalties? Knowledge is power, and it can help you navigate the legal system with confidence.

Lawyer Up

If there's even a chance of legal trouble, have a lawyer on your side. Ideally, someone experienced in activism or civil rights. They can guide you, represent you, and help minimize the damage.

Support Networks

You don't have to face legal battles alone. Many organizations provide support for activists, from legal aid to fundraising for bail. Reach out, connect, and build a network before you need it.

Dealing with Disapproval from Allies

This is where things get tricky. When your allies turn against you, it can feel like a betrayal. But it's important to remember that disagreements are inevitable in any movement.

Understand Their Perspective

Before you react, try to understand where they're coming from. Are they worried about public perception? Do they disagree with your methods? Are they under pressure from others?

Open a Dialogue

Don't let resentment fester. Talk to your allies, listen to their concerns, and share your perspective. Sometimes, a simple conversation can mend the rift.

Stay True to Your Values

At the end of the day, you can't please everyone. If you believe in your deed and your message, stand by it. Your allies may come around—or they may not. Either way, you have to stay true to yourself.

Turning Backlash into Opportunity

Here's the thing about backlash: it can be a gift, if you know how to use it. Every angry headline, every outraged tweet, every debate on the evening news—they're all opportunities to amplify your message.

Lean Into the Controversy

If people are talking about your action, they're already paying attention. Use that attention to highlight your cause, clarify your message, and keep the conversation going.

Rally Your Supporters

Backlash can galvanize your supporters, uniting them against a common enemy. Use the momentum to build your base, raise funds, or organize follow-up actions.

Learn and Adapt

Every action is a learning experience. Use the backlash to refine your approach, strengthen your strategy, and prepare for the next battle.

Case Studies: Backlash in Action

The Civil Rights Movement

The Civil Rights Movement faced immense backlash, from violent mobs to legal persecution. But leaders like Martin Luther King Jr. used that backlash to expose the brutality of segregation and rally support for their cause.

Greta Thunberg

When Greta Thunberg began her climate strike, she faced intense criticism from politicians, pundits, and the public. But instead of retreating, she leaned into the controversy, using it to amplify her message and inspire a global movement.

Final Thoughts

Backlash is a storm, and storms can be terrifying. But they can also be cleansing, clearing the air and carving new paths. If you face it head-on—with preparation, resilience, and a clear sense of purpose—you'll not only survive, but thrive.

Because in the end, backlash isn't just a sign that you've made waves. It's a sign that you've made a difference.

Chapter 25: Digital Propaganda of the Deed

Let's start with a scene we all know too well: the hum of a laptop, the faint glow of a screen in a darkened room, fingers tapping out a rhythm faster than a heartbeat. It's the digital age's version of a clandestine meeting in the dead of night. Except this isn't the plotting of old, with whispers and candles flickering on damp stone walls. No, this is a revolution of ones and zeroes—a battle fought not with swords or bombs, but with keystrokes and data packets.

Welcome to the world of digital propaganda of the deed, where the theater of action has moved online. It's quieter, sure. No grand explosions, no echoing gunshots. But don't mistake silence for impotence. In this realm, the drama plays out in headlines and hashtags, and its heroes and villains are the ones who wield code as both shield and sword.

The Rise of Cyberactivism

Before we dig into the nitty-gritty, let's set the stage. Digital propaganda of the deed didn't sprout from nowhere. It evolved alongside the internet, from the moment we first learned to connect across continents with the click of a button. It's a natural extension of a world where information is currency, and where the most profound truths and the darkest secrets live in servers and clouds.

PROPAGANDA OF THE DEED

Why the Internet Changed Everything

Think back to the earliest forms of activism. Pamphlets smuggled across borders. Speeches shouted from street corners. The occasional underground newspaper, read by a flickering lantern. Information was slow, labor-intensive, and easy to suppress. Burn the presses, imprison the printers, and you could silence a movement.

The internet changed all that. It made information fluid, fast, and nearly impossible to contain. It gave power to the anonymous, the marginalized, and the furious. And for those looking to shake the system, it provided a new stage for their deeds.

Hacking as a Modern-Day Molotov Cocktail

If traditional propaganda of the deed is about creating a spectacle that sparks change, then hacking is its digital counterpart. It's disruptive. It's dramatic. And when done right, it's impossible to ignore.

The Anonymous Era

Let's talk about Anonymous, the faceless collective with their Guy Fawkes masks and rallying cry of *"We are legion."* In 2008, they took on the Church of Scientology in a campaign called *Project Chanology*. It started as a simple act of defiance: leaking internal videos and documents to expose the church's secrets. But it quickly snowballed into something much bigger—protests, media attention, and a global reckoning with the shadowy power of Scientology.

Anonymous didn't invent hacking for activism, but they turned it into performance art. Their deeds weren't just about the information they uncovered; they were about the spectacle of the uncovering.

Hacktivism Today

Fast-forward to today, and hacktivism is alive and well. Groups like LulzSec and CyberBerkut have kept the tradition alive, using data breaches and website defacements to send their messages. And then there's WikiLeaks, the infamous platform that made headlines with its massive leaks of classified information.

Whether you see them as heroes or villains, there's no denying their impact. When hackers hit their targets, the world takes notice.

Leaks: Truth as a Weapon

If hacking is the blow to the system, then leaks are the aftermath—the smoldering ruins that force everyone to confront uncomfortable truths. And in a world where information is power, leaks have become one of the most potent forms of digital propaganda of the deed.

Edward Snowden: The Whistleblower's Whistleblower

You can't talk about leaks without mentioning Edward Snowden. In 2013, the former NSA contractor turned the world upside down when he exposed the U.S. government's mass surveillance programs. His revelations weren't just shocking—they were revolutionary. They forced us to rethink our relationship with privacy, technology, and the state.

Snowden's act wasn't violent, but it was explosive in every other sense of the word. It was a modern-day manifesto, written not in blood, but in meticulously documented files.

The Pandora Papers and Beyond

Snowden isn't alone. From the Panama Papers to the Pandora Papers, leaks have become a go-to weapon for activists, journalists, and whistleblowers alike. Each one is a digital dagger aimed at the heart of corruption, secrecy, and abuse of power.

Cyberactivism Without the Hack

Not every digital deed requires hacking or leaking classified documents. Sometimes, the most effective acts are the simplest.

Hashtag Activism

Think about #BlackLivesMatter, #MeToo, and #ArabSpring. These weren't just social media trends—they were movements, fueled by millions of voices joining together in a digital chorus.

A hashtag might seem small, almost insignificant. But when it's attached to a powerful story or an undeniable truth, it can spread like wildfire, igniting conversations and inspiring action in ways that no single act ever could.

Digital Occupations

Then there are digital occupations, where activists take over online spaces to make their point. In 2020, TikTok users and K-pop fans coordinated a campaign to flood a Trump rally's online RSVP system with fake sign-ups, leaving thousands of seats empty. It was a small, symbolic act, but it sent a big message.

The Theater of the Online Spectacle

One of the most fascinating things about digital propaganda of the deed is its theatricality. These acts aren't just about achieving a specific goal—they're about creating a narrative, a story that captivates, shocks, and inspires.

Memes as Propaganda

Memes might seem trivial, but they're a powerful tool in the digital activist's arsenal. A well-crafted meme can distill complex ideas into bite-sized, shareable content that spreads like a virus. It's humor and outrage wrapped up in a neat little package, designed to bypass logic and hit straight at the gut.

The Virality Factor

Virality is the holy grail of digital deeds. The more people see your act, the greater its impact. But virality isn't just about luck—it's about understanding your audience, timing your release, and crafting a message that resonates on a visceral level.

The Risks of Digital Action

Of course, the digital stage comes with its own set of dangers. The internet might feel anonymous, but in reality, it's anything but.

Surveillance and Doxxing

Governments and corporations have become increasingly adept at monitoring online activity. Activists who think they're safe behind a screen often find themselves unmasked, doxxed, or even arrested.

Echo Chambers and Misinformation

Then there's the risk of your message being distorted or co-opted. The internet is a breeding ground for misinformation, and even the most well-intentioned acts can spiral out of control if you're not careful.

Lessons for Digital Activists

If you're thinking about stepping onto the digital stage, here are a few things to keep in mind:

1. **Stay Anonymous**
   Protect your identity. Use encryption, VPNs, and secure communication channels. The less they know about you, the harder it is to shut you down.
2. **Be Strategic**
   Digital deeds aren't just about making noise—they're about making an impact. Plan your actions carefully, and think about the long-term consequences.
3. **Control the Narrative**

In the digital world, perception is reality. Make sure your message is clear, compelling, and impossible to ignore.

4. **Build a Network**
   You're stronger together. Connect with like-minded individuals and organizations, and work as a team to amplify your impact.

The Future of Digital Propaganda of the Deed

As technology continues to evolve, so too will the tactics of digital activism. Artificial intelligence, blockchain, and even virtual reality could open up new possibilities for disrupting the system and inspiring change.

But one thing will remain constant: the power of action, of deeds that speak louder than words. Whether it's a leaked document, a viral hashtag, or a hacked server, the digital stage will continue to be a battleground for the soul of society.

And if you're brave enough to step into the spotlight, to take your stand in this strange, glowing world, just remember: every keystroke is a ripple, and every ripple has the potential to become a wave.

Chapter 26: Climate Activism in the 21st Century

The Earth is burning.

Not figuratively, not poetically—literally. Look out your window, and you might see blue skies, a gentle breeze. But somewhere out there, the forests are ablaze, the ice is dripping into the sea, and the oceans are swallowing entire nations. The end of the world doesn't come with a bang. It comes with the slow, steady rise of the thermometer, ticking upward like a time bomb.

And in the face of all this, people are still shopping for new SUVs. Still tossing plastic bottles into the trash. Still pretending we've got time.

This is where climate activists come in.

The climate crisis isn't just a disaster—it's a challenge, a problem so big and overwhelming that it demands a response as dramatic as the crisis itself. Enter propaganda of the deed. In the 21st century, climate activism has become one of the most potent arenas for bold, symbolic actions designed to shake the world awake.

A Planet in Peril

Let's start with the stakes. Climate change isn't a distant problem, something that might happen to our grandchildren someday. It's here, right now, reshaping the planet in ways we can't ignore. Hurricanes are battering coastal cities. Heatwaves are cooking entire regions. And the people who suffer the most are always the ones who did the least to cause it.

So, what do you do when the science is undeniable, but the action is nonexistent? How do you fight a problem this vast, this urgent, this existential?

The answer, for some, is simple: you make people pay attention. You disrupt. You confront. You act.

The Rise of Climate Direct Action

Climate activism has been around for decades, but in recent years, it's become sharper, louder, and more radical. Groups like Extinction Rebellion, Greenpeace, and Fridays for Future aren't just organizing rallies or writing op-eds—they're shutting down highways, scaling oil rigs, and gluing themselves to priceless works of art.

Why Now?

The answer to "Why now?" is as obvious as a thermometer spiking past 100 degrees Fahrenheit in October. The climate clock is ticking, and the window for action is closing. Scientists warn we have only a few years left to avert the worst effects of climate change. For activists, this isn't just a political issue—it's a moral emergency.

When traditional methods—petitions, marches, polite lobbying—fail to move the needle, more dramatic measures become not just an option but a necessity.

PROPAGANDA OF THE DEED

The Tactics of Climate Activists

Climate propaganda of the deed comes in many forms. Some are loud and theatrical; others are quiet but deeply symbolic. Let's break them down.

Shutting It Down

One of the most visible tactics is disruption. Think of it as throwing sand into the gears of the machine. Protesters block roads, airports, and oil pipelines, forcing the world to pay attention to their message, if only to clear the way.

Take Extinction Rebellion, for example. In 2019, the group brought central London to a standstill, occupying bridges and streets for days. Their actions didn't just inconvenience commuters—they sparked a national conversation about the climate crisis.

Targeting Fossil Fuel Infrastructure

Another powerful tactic is going straight to the source. Activists have sabotaged oil pipelines, chained themselves to coal trains, and even boarded drilling rigs in the middle of the ocean. These actions aren't just symbolic—they're also practical, slowing down the machinery of environmental destruction.

One infamous example is the Valve Turners, a group of activists who, in 2016, manually shut off pipelines carrying tar sands oil across the United States. Their message was clear: if governments won't stop fossil fuels, the people will.

Art and Iconoclasm

In recent years, climate activists have turned to art as a battleground. Groups like Just Stop Oil have made headlines by targeting famous artworks, throwing soup at Van Gogh's *Sunflowers* or gluing themselves to frames in prestigious galleries. The goal? To provoke outrage and force the public to confront the absurdity of valuing art over a dying planet.

Self-Sacrifice

Some acts are quieter but no less powerful. Hunger strikes, self-immolation, and other forms of personal sacrifice have long been tools of protest. In 2022, a climate activist named Wynn Bruce set himself on fire on the steps of the U.S. Supreme Court—a horrifying act meant to draw attention to the urgency of the crisis.

The Power of Symbolism

Every deed has a message. In the case of climate activism, the message is often stark and uncompromising: "This is an emergency." The actions are designed to cut through the noise, to shake people out of their complacency.

Theatrics and Spectacle

Climate propaganda of the deed thrives on spectacle. It's not enough to make a point—you have to make it unforgettable. When activists glue themselves to famous paintings or dangle from suspension bridges, they're creating a visual image that sticks in the public's mind, long after the police have dragged them away.

PROPAGANDA OF THE DEED

The Moral High Ground

Climate activists also understand the power of moral clarity. Their actions are rooted in a simple truth: the planet is dying, and the people in power aren't doing enough to save it. By putting their bodies on the line, activists position themselves as the righteous underdogs, fighting against overwhelming odds.

Criticism and Controversy

Of course, not everyone sees these actions as heroic. Climate activists face intense backlash, not just from corporations and governments but also from ordinary people who feel inconvenienced by their tactics.

The Public's Reaction

When protesters block a busy highway, the people stuck in traffic don't always respond with gratitude. Critics argue that these actions alienate potential allies, turning public opinion against the movement.

But activists counter that disruption is the whole point. If the climate crisis isn't inconvenient, if it doesn't force people to stop and think, then it's all too easy to ignore.

The Question of Effectiveness

Then there's the question of whether these deeds actually make a difference. Does throwing soup at a painting reduce carbon emissions? Does gluing yourself to a bridge stop global warming?

The answer, according to activists, lies in the ripple effect. These actions might not solve the problem directly, but they spark conversations, shift cultural norms, and put pressure on governments and corporations to act.

The Intersection of Local and Global

One of the unique challenges of climate activism is its scale. The climate crisis is a global problem, but it manifests in deeply local ways—wildfires in California, floods in Bangladesh, droughts in sub-Saharan Africa.

Global Movements

Groups like Fridays for Future, led by Greta Thunberg, have managed to bridge this gap, creating a global movement that feels personal and urgent. Their weekly school strikes, which began with a single teenager outside the Swedish parliament, have grown into a worldwide phenomenon.

Local Heroes

At the same time, local activists are on the front lines of the crisis, fighting battles that might never make the headlines. From Indigenous groups defending their land against oil companies to communities rallying against toxic waste dumps, these grassroots efforts are just as vital as the global movements.

The Road Ahead

The fight against climate change is far from over. If anything, the stakes are higher than ever. As the crisis deepens, climate activism will only become more urgent, more radical, and more creative.

Innovations in Activism

The future of climate propaganda of the deed might involve new technologies—think drones dropping banners over corporate headquarters or virtual reality experiences that immerse people in the realities of a warming planet.

The Role of Solidarity

Ultimately, the success of these actions depends on solidarity. Climate activism isn't just about individual deeds—it's about building a movement, a wave of people who refuse to accept the status quo.

Final Thoughts

The earth is burning, yes. But it's also fighting back. Every protest, every blockade, every symbolic deed is a spark of hope, a reminder that the battle isn't over.

And if the climate activists of the 21st century have anything to say about it, the story of this planet won't end in flames. It will end in action.

Chapter 27: Intersectionality and Inclusive Action

The thing about oppression is that it rarely comes alone. It sneaks into your life like a stranger with bad intentions, bringing its friends along for the ride. Racism might shuffle in first, pulling up a chair and getting comfortable. Then sexism walks through the door, followed by ableism, homophobia, and classism, each dragging their own dirty luggage behind them.

Before you know it, you're surrounded, overwhelmed by the sheer weight of it all.

The human experience is messy like that. People aren't just one thing. They're not just women, or Black, or queer, or disabled, or poor. They're all those things at once, layered and complex, like a painting where every brushstroke adds another dimension. And when oppression works this way—layered, interwoven—you better believe that activism needs to do the same.

That's where intersectionality comes in.

Coined by Kimberlé Crenshaw, a legal scholar with a knack for seeing what the rest of the world missed, intersectionality is about understanding how systems of oppression overlap and interact. It's about seeing the whole person—not just the labels society slaps on them—and fighting for justice in a way that reflects that messy, beautiful complexity.

In the world of propaganda of the deed, intersectionality isn't just a buzzword. It's a roadmap, a way to craft actions that don't just tackle one issue in isolation but challenge the entire system of oppression. It's about saying, "We see you. All of you. And we're fighting for all of you."

A Web of Oppression

Imagine a spider's web stretched taut between two trees. Each thread is a different form of oppression—racism, sexism, homophobia, ableism, classism, you name it. Tug on one thread, and the whole web trembles. That's how oppression works. You can't dismantle one part of it without affecting the rest.

But here's the catch: most movements, most acts of resistance, tend to focus on a single thread. They pick their battles—fight for women's rights, or labor rights, or environmental justice—and hope the rest will sort itself out.

It's not enough.

When activists ignore the intersections, they risk leaving people behind. A women's rights movement that doesn't address racism? That leaves women of color out in the cold. A labor movement that ignores gender? That sidelines the unique struggles of working-class women and queer folks.

Intersectionality is about refusing to leave anyone behind. It's about recognizing that the fight for justice isn't a series of isolated battles but one interconnected war.

Crafting Inclusive Deeds

So, how do you turn this philosophy into action? How do you craft deeds that reflect the complexity of the world we're fighting for?

1. Know Your Audience

The first step is simple: listen. Talk to the communities you want to fight for. Understand their struggles, their fears, their dreams. It's not enough to have good intentions—you need to have good information.

Take the Dakota Access Pipeline protests, for example. At first glance, it might seem like a straightforward environmental issue—protecting water, fighting climate change. But for the Standing Rock Sioux Tribe, it was about so much more. It was about sovereignty, about centuries of broken treaties and stolen land. The protests weren't just about water—they were about survival, about dignity.

When you know your audience, your actions can speak directly to their struggles. They can resonate in ways that no abstract principle ever could.

2. Build Coalitions

Intersectionality is about bringing people together. It's about recognizing that we're stronger when we fight as one.

Look at the Black Lives Matter movement. At its core, it's about racial justice, about ending police violence against Black communities. But it's also about economic justice, about LGBTQ+ rights, about dismantling the prison-industrial complex. BLM didn't just build a movement—it built a coalition, a broad, inclusive alliance of people who understood that their struggles were interconnected.

When you craft a deed, think about who you can bring to the table. Who else has a stake in this fight? Whose voices need to be heard?

3. Make It Visible

Visibility is power. A deed that no one sees might as well not have happened.

But here's the trick: visibility doesn't just mean getting on the news. It means making sure the right people are visible. It means centering the voices of the most marginalized, amplifying their stories, and putting their struggles front and center.

Think about the 2017 Women's March. It was a powerful moment, a sea of pink hats stretching as far as the eye could see. But it also faced criticism for sidelining women of color, for failing to address the intersections of race, class, and gender. The lesson? Visibility without intersectionality is hollow.

Examples of Inclusive Action

Stonewall and the Birth of Pride

The Stonewall Riots of 1969 weren't just about gay rights. They were about liberation in its rawest, most intersectional form. Led by trans women of color like Marsha P. Johnson and Sylvia Rivera, Stonewall wasn't just a fight against police brutality—it was a fight against every system that told queer people they were less than human.

The riots were messy, chaotic, and imperfect. But they were also inclusive, a testament to the power of standing together.

The Fight for $15

The Fight for $15, a campaign for a living wage, is another example of intersectional activism done right. It's not just about raising wages—it's about addressing the intersections of race, gender, and class. It's about lifting up the working poor, the single mothers, the immigrant workers who keep the economy running but can barely make ends meet.

By centering the voices of the most marginalized, the Fight for $15 has become more than a labor movement—it's a movement for dignity, for equality.

The Challenges of Intersectional Action

Of course, it's not easy. Intersectionality is messy, and inclusive action comes with its own set of challenges.

Balancing Competing Priorities

When you're trying to address multiple forms of oppression at once, it's easy to get overwhelmed. How do you prioritize?

How do you make sure one issue doesn't overshadow the others?

The key is to remember that intersectionality isn't about solving everything all at once. It's about recognizing the connections, about seeing the bigger picture even as you focus on the task at hand.

Internal Tensions

Movements are made up of people, and people don't always get along. There will be disagreements, conflicts, moments when the coalition feels like it's falling apart.

But that's okay. Conflict is part of the process. It's how you grow, how you learn, how you build something stronger.

The Future of Intersectional Action

The world is changing. The fights of the 21st century—climate change, systemic racism, economic inequality—demand a new kind of activism, one that reflects the complexity of the world we live in.

Intersectionality isn't just a buzzword. It's the future. It's the blueprint for a new kind of resistance, one that refuses to leave anyone behind.

So, when you craft your deeds, remember this: the web of oppression is vast and tangled, but so is the web of liberation. Every thread you pull, every connection you make, brings us one step closer to a world where justice isn't just a dream—it's a reality.

BRADLEY HALL

And isn't that worth fighting for?

Chapter 28: The Line Between Art and Action

There's a peculiar thing about a line. You think it's something solid, something you can hold onto—until you try. Then, it slips through your fingers, becoming a smear, a suggestion, a whisper of what you thought it was. The line between art and action is like that. It teases you, tempts you, but when you look closer, it isn't really there at all.

If you've ever stood in a crowd during a protest and felt your chest rattle with the roar of voices—if you've watched a banner unfold with colors so bold they feel like a punch to the gut—you've already felt it. That thin, gossamer thread where art and action intertwine, where a deed becomes something greater, something mythic.

Propaganda of the deed doesn't just work on the practical plane. It doesn't just disrupt, ignite, or provoke—it leaves an image burned into the collective consciousness, seared there like a brand. And that image? That's where art takes over.

This chapter is about that liminal space, that knife's edge where the symbolic merges with the literal. Because, whether you're holding a brush or a Molotov cocktail, whether you're writing a manifesto or spray-painting a slogan onto the side of a building, you're performing something greater than yourself.

And the world? It's watching.

When a Message Becomes a Medium

Let's start with a question: what makes something art? Is it the creator's intent? The skill in execution? Or is it the way it makes you feel, the way it reaches deep inside and shakes you like a leaf in the wind?

Now, flip the coin. What makes something an action? The outcome? The effect it has on the world?

Most propaganda of the deed lives somewhere between the two. It's art as much as it's action, action as much as it's art. Take the act of kneeling during a national anthem. It doesn't destroy property, it doesn't directly change laws—but it burns. It burns in the eyes of those who see it, in the hearts of those who feel it.

The deed becomes a canvas. The message becomes a brushstroke.

Consider Colin Kaepernick's protest during the NFL games in 2016. Was it art? Was it action? It didn't matter what you called it because the image—his body, knelt in defiance, in grief, in power—was the deed. It echoed through living rooms and newsrooms, through angry Facebook comment sections and whispered conversations.

It was symbolic. It was real.

And it hit harder than a thousand words ever could.

The Anatomy of Symbolism

Here's the thing about symbols: they're cheap to make and priceless in effect.

When Rosa Parks refused to give up her seat, she wasn't the first person to defy segregation laws. Others had done it before her. But her act became iconic because it was perfectly placed in time and perfectly executed in simplicity. A woman, tired after a long day's work, sitting in quiet defiance. It was an image that spoke louder than speeches and sermons, a perfect piece of living art.

Now, think about protest art. Murals painted on city walls, like the Black Lives Matter street murals that stretched across the asphalt during the summer of 2020. Were they just art? Or were they deeds, meant to claim space, to provoke, to declare ownership of a society that too often denies the humanity of Black lives?

The power lies in their duality. A mural is both static and active. It doesn't move, but it moves *you*.

Propaganda of the deed thrives on this duality. A good deed doesn't just do something—it says something.

Performance in Protest

Now let's step into the world of performance art. This is where the line between art and action gets particularly blurry.

Take Pussy Riot, the Russian feminist punk collective. In 2012, they performed an anti-Putin "punk prayer" inside Moscow's Cathedral of Christ the Savior. The act was chaotic, raw, and undeniably artistic, but it was also an act of rebellion, a middle finger to a regime that thrives on silence and conformity.

For this performance, they were arrested and imprisoned. But here's the kicker: the power of their deed didn't end in that cathedral. It spread. The image of them, clad in bright balaclavas, screaming defiance in a holy space, became iconic. It was performance as protest, protest as performance.

The same could be said of Greta Thunberg's weekly climate strikes. Her lone figure sitting outside the Swedish parliament, holding a hand-painted sign, was both a performance and a deed. Her silence spoke volumes, her stillness screamed urgency.

Both acts—Pussy Riot's riotous spectacle and Thunberg's quiet defiance—blurred the line between art and action, creating something far more potent than either could be on its own.

Art as a Weapon

When art is wielded as a weapon, it cuts deeper than most deeds ever could. Think of the anti-apartheid posters that spread across South Africa, their bold colors and stark imagery carving a path through decades of systemic racism. Or the haunting photographs of Emmett Till's open casket, which turned a mother's grief into a rallying cry for the civil rights movement.

These weren't just images—they were declarations of war, propaganda of the deed in visual form.

Then there's Banksy, the enigmatic street artist whose works appear like whispers in the night. His pieces are subversive, often playful, but they carry the weight of a sledgehammer. When he painted a mural on the West Bank barrier—a girl floating over the wall with a bunch of balloons—it wasn't just art. It was an act of defiance, a challenge to a structure meant to divide and oppress.

Art like this doesn't just reflect the world—it reshapes it.

The Dangers of Performative Protest

But here's where it gets tricky. Not every symbolic act lands the way it's intended.

There's a fine line between performance as protest and protest as performance. When the focus shifts too far toward spectacle, the message can get lost. Worse, it can feel hollow, a cheap stunt rather than a meaningful action.

Think of the Pepsi ad featuring Kendall Jenner, where a staged protest was reduced to a marketing gimmick. It tried to capture the aesthetic of resistance without any of the substance. The result was a backlash so fierce it became a case study in how not to blend art and action.

The lesson here is simple: the deed must come first. The art, the symbolism, must serve the action—not the other way around.

Crafting a Hybrid Power

So, how do you walk that tightrope? How do you craft a deed that is both action and art, both symbolic and substantive?

1. Be Authentic

Authenticity is the backbone of effective propaganda of the deed. If your action feels contrived, if it feels like a stunt, people will see right through it.

2. Aim for Simplicity

The most powerful symbols are often the simplest. A kneeling figure. A raised fist. A single, bold word painted on a wall.

3. Make It Resonate

Your deed should speak to something universal, something primal. It should tap into emotions that words alone can't reach.

The Legacy of Symbolic Deeds

In the end, the line between art and action doesn't matter as much as the impact. When you think about the Boston Tea Party, do you see it as a piece of political theater or a revolutionary act? Does it matter?

What matters is the image: crates of tea splashing into the harbor, a protest so theatrical it burned its way into history.

The same goes for every successful act of propaganda of the deed. It's not about where it lands on the spectrum between art and action. It's about how it makes people feel, what it inspires them to do.

Because at the end of the day, art and action are two sides of the same coin. Both are about transformation, about turning the ordinary into the extraordinary, about making people see the world—not as it is, but as it could be.

And that? That's where the real magic happens.

Chapter 29: Scaling Up

Movements don't erupt fully formed like Athena from the head of Zeus. They start small, usually with a spark so tiny it's almost imperceptible. A lone figure holding a sign in a cold wind, a whispered idea over coffee, or a single daring act that echoes in a way no one could have predicted. Scaling up from these humble beginnings into a force that shakes the foundations of society—that's the real magic trick.

But let's be honest: scaling up is messy. It's like trying to teach a bonfire to behave. You want it to grow big enough to be seen from the mountaintop, but not so wild it burns the forest down. It's a dance between inspiration and organization, between chaos and control.

And if you're lucky, if you're smart, if the gods of momentum smile on you, that spark turns into something unstoppable.

The Anatomy of a Spark

Every mass movement starts with a spark, but not every spark becomes a wildfire. Why?

The key lies in resonance. Take Rosa Parks again, sitting on that Montgomery bus. Her refusal wasn't the first act of defiance against segregation, but it was the right act at the right time, in the right place, performed by the right person. Her action didn't just challenge the system—it sent ripples through it.

Think of your small action as a stone dropped into a pond. The initial splash isn't the whole story. It's the ripples, the way they spread outward, that changes the surface of the water. Scaling up means turning those ripples into waves—and waves into tsunamis.

But here's the catch: for that to happen, the pond has to be ready.

The Ecosystem of Change

Scaling up doesn't happen in a vacuum. You need fertile ground, a society primed for change.

The Civil Rights Movement wasn't born in Montgomery or Birmingham or even Washington, D.C. It was born in the silent frustration of millions of Black Americans living under Jim Crow. It was nurtured by the whispers of grandparents telling their grandchildren, *This isn't right.*

When Parks took her stand—or rather, her seat—she didn't create the movement. She activated it.

The same holds true for every act of propaganda of the deed. A single action, no matter how bold, won't do much unless it plugs into a larger context, a collective energy waiting for ignition. Scaling up isn't about you. It's about the movement you're trying to grow.

The Mechanics of Momentum

Momentum is a tricky thing. It's not just about the size of the action—it's about the timing, the amplification, and the follow-through.

1. Timing Is Everything

You could stage the most brilliant act of protest in the world, but if it lands at the wrong time, it'll sink like a stone.

Think about Greta Thunberg. Her climate strike in 2018 wasn't the first call to action against the climate crisis, but it came at a moment when the world was starting to wake up to the urgency of the problem. The timing turned her solitary act into a global movement.

2. Amplification

Your deed needs a megaphone. That megaphone might be traditional media, social media, or even word of mouth.

The Black Lives Matter movement exploded in 2014 because of a combination of grassroots organization and viral social media campaigns. Hashtags like #BlackLivesMatter turned individual tragedies into rallying cries, ensuring that small actions like marches and vigils were seen and felt worldwide.

3. Follow-Through

A spark is nothing without kindling. Scaling up requires a plan, a way to build on the initial energy of your action.

Look at the Occupy Wall Street movement. It began with a single act—protesters occupying Zuccotti Park in 2011—but it faltered because it lacked clear objectives. Contrast that with the Civil Rights Movement, which combined bold deeds with a relentless focus on legislative change.

Scaling Through Storytelling

Here's a secret: people don't follow movements. They follow stories.

Every successful movement has a narrative that hooks people, that makes them feel like they're part of something bigger than themselves. Your small action is the opening chapter of that story. Scaling up means writing the next chapters in a way that keeps people turning the pages.

Think about the Women's Suffrage Movement. Its narrative was simple but powerful: women deserve a voice. Every march, every hunger strike, every window smashed added to that story, creating a crescendo that was impossible to ignore.

Your deed, no matter how small, is a seed. If the story surrounding it is strong enough, it can grow into a forest.

The Role of Leadership

Scaling up isn't just about the crowd—it's about the people guiding it.

Leadership in a movement is like conducting an orchestra. You don't have to play every instrument yourself, but you do have to set the tempo, keep everyone in tune, and make sure the music is building toward something.

Take Martin Luther King Jr. His strength wasn't just in his rhetoric—it was in his ability to unify a fractured movement, to channel a thousand small actions into a single, unstoppable force.

But leadership doesn't always have to be centralized. Look at the decentralized structure of Extinction Rebellion. By giving power to local chapters, they've managed to scale up without losing momentum.

Harnessing Technology

In the 21st century, technology is the great equalizer. A single tweet, a single video, can turn a small deed into a global phenomenon.

The Arab Spring in 2011 is a case in point. Protests that began in Tunisia spread across the Middle East, fueled by social media. Platforms like Facebook and Twitter didn't just amplify the message—they created a sense of solidarity among protesters in different countries, turning isolated actions into a regional uprising.

Scaling up in the digital age means knowing how to use these tools effectively. It's not enough to have a message—you need to know how to make it go viral.

The Risks of Growing Too Fast

Scaling up isn't without its dangers. Growth can be intoxicating, but it can also be destabilizing.

Movements that grow too fast often lose focus. They become vulnerable to infiltration, co-optation, and infighting. The larger the crowd, the harder it is to maintain a unified vision.

Consider the Occupy movement again. Its rapid growth was both its greatest strength and its Achilles' heel. Without clear leadership or goals, the movement struggled to channel its energy into lasting change.

The lesson? Scaling up is about more than numbers. It's about maintaining the integrity of your vision as you grow.

Case Study: The Montgomery Bus Boycott

Let's break this down with an example. The Montgomery Bus Boycott in 1955 started with a single act: Rosa Parks' arrest.

That act sparked a boycott that lasted over a year, involving tens of thousands of people. But the boycott didn't succeed on momentum alone. It succeeded because it was meticulously planned, with leaders organizing carpools, spreading the word through churches, and maintaining discipline among participants.

The boycott scaled up because it combined bold action with careful organization. It wasn't just a spark—it was a fire carefully tended until it burned hot enough to melt the chains of segregation.

From Local to Global

Scaling up often means expanding beyond your initial community. A local protest can become a national movement, and a national movement can become a global one.

Think about Fridays for Future, the climate movement started by Greta Thunberg. What began with a single teenager outside the Swedish parliament grew into a global phenomenon, with millions of young people joining climate strikes around the world.

The key was scalability. Thunberg's message was universal, her action easy to replicate. Scaling up means creating a blueprint that others can follow.

The Legacy of Scaling Up

Scaling up isn't just about making your action bigger—it's about making it matter. It's about taking a small, symbolic deed and turning it into a movement that changes the world.

The Boston Tea Party. The Salt March. The March on Washington. All of these began with small acts that scaled into something monumental.

Your spark might be small now. It might feel insignificant. But if you tend it, if you feed it with the right fuel, if you share its light with others, it can grow into a blaze that lights the way for generations to come.

Because in the end, scaling up is about belief—the belief that one small act, one tiny spark, can set the world on fire.

Chapter 30: Your Role in the Struggle

S omewhere out there, the world is waiting for you.

It doesn't know your name yet, doesn't know what you've done or what you're going to do. It hasn't heard your footsteps on the pavement or your voice echoing in the hallways of power. Not yet. But it's waiting. The way the air waits before a storm. The way the ground waits for spring.

The struggle—the real struggle—doesn't belong to some ancient storybook of revolutions and rebellions. It isn't locked away in the 19th century with Bakunin or Pisacane, or even the 20th century with King and Malcolm and Mandela. It's here. It's now. And whether you want to or not, whether you believe it or not, you're part of it.

This chapter isn't about history. It isn't about tactics or theory or how to hold a protest sign so it doesn't break in the wind. This chapter is about you.

The Reluctant Hero

Most people don't start out thinking they'll change the world. They don't wake up one morning, pour a cup of coffee, and say, *You know, I think I'll take down the system today.*

No, it sneaks up on you.

Maybe you're sitting in traffic one day and see a homeless veteran on the corner, holding a sign that says, *Anything helps.* Maybe you're scrolling through your phone and see a photo of a starving polar bear on a melting iceberg. Or maybe you're standing in line at the grocery store, watching the mom in front of you put back the milk because she can't afford it.

And something shifts.

It's not like a lightning bolt. It's more like a slow burn. A whisper that grows louder every time you look at the world around you. *This isn't right. This isn't how it's supposed to be.*

The truth is, most people never act on that whisper. They drown it out with work and bills and reruns of their favorite shows. They tell themselves, *Someone else will fix it. Someone smarter, braver, stronger than me.*

But here's the secret: no one's coming.

There is no cavalry riding over the hill. No superhero swinging in to save the day. It's just us. You, me, and everyone else who's ever felt that whisper in their gut.

Ordinary People, Extraordinary Deeds

Every movement in history was built by people like you. Ordinary people who decided they couldn't wait anymore.

The kids who sat at the lunch counters in Greensboro? They were college students. They had exams to study for and part-time jobs to work. But they sat down anyway.

The farmers who marched with Gandhi during the Salt March? They weren't soldiers or politicians. They were just people who wanted to make a living without being crushed under the heel of empire.

The mothers who marched in Buenos Aires during Argentina's Dirty War, holding pictures of their disappeared children? They weren't radicals or revolutionaries. They were grieving parents who refused to stay silent.

They weren't special. They weren't chosen. They just showed up. And showing up—over and over again—is how change happens.

The Fear That Holds You Back

Let's talk about fear for a minute. Because it's real.

The fear of sticking your neck out, of stepping into the unknown. The fear of failing, of looking stupid, of losing what little you have.

That fear is what keeps most people on the sidelines. It whispers in your ear, *Who do you think you are? What difference could you possibly make?*

But here's the thing about fear: it's a liar.

Fear wants you to believe that you're alone, that your voice doesn't matter, that the system is too big and too powerful to fight. But history tells a different story.

The Berlin Wall didn't fall because one person swung a sledgehammer at it. It fell because millions of people across East Germany, Poland, Hungary, and beyond decided they'd had enough.

The Civil Rights Act didn't pass because Martin Luther King Jr. gave a great speech. It passed because millions of nameless, faceless people marched and protested and organized and refused to back down.

Fear is the voice that tells you to stay small. But courage—that's the voice that tells you to stand up anyway.

Finding Your Place

You don't have to save the world all at once.

Maybe your role in the struggle is local, helping your community fight for clean water or better schools. Maybe it's online, amplifying the voices of those on the frontlines. Maybe it's in your workplace, organizing for fair wages or safer conditions.

The point isn't where you start. The point is that you start.

Find what matters to you. Maybe it's climate change. Maybe it's racial justice. Maybe it's healthcare or housing or ending endless wars. Whatever it is, find the thing that makes your blood boil, the thing that makes you say, *Not on my watch.*

And then get to work.

The Power of Small Actions

PROPAGANDA OF THE DEED

You don't need a grand plan. You don't need to organize a march on Washington or chain yourself to a tree.

Start small. Volunteer at a local food bank. Write a letter to your senator. Show up at a city council meeting. Join a group that's already doing the work.

Small actions add up. One person becomes ten, ten becomes a hundred, a hundred becomes a movement.

Remember Greta Thunberg, sitting alone outside the Swedish parliament with her little sign? She didn't know she was starting a global movement. She was just a kid who couldn't stand to sit in silence anymore.

You don't have to be perfect. You don't have to have all the answers. You just have to take that first step.

The Ripple Effect

Here's the thing about action: it's contagious.

When you stand up, you give other people permission to stand up too. When you speak out, you remind people that they have a voice.

Your courage becomes their courage. Your deed becomes their inspiration.

And before you know it, the ripples you started have turned into waves.

The Legacy You Leave Behind

Someday, long after you're gone, someone will look back on the world you helped shape.

Maybe they'll sit under a tree you planted, drink clean water from a river you fought to protect, or walk through a city where equality isn't just a dream but a reality.

They won't know your name. They won't know the nights you spent lying awake, wondering if you were doing enough. They won't know the fear you felt, the sacrifices you made.

But they'll know the world you left behind.

And that, in the end, is what it's all about.

The Call to Action

So here's the question: what will you do?

You've read the history. You've learned the tactics. You've seen the risks and the rewards.

Now it's up to you.

You can let the world pass you by, let someone else fight the battles, let someone else take the risks. Or you can decide, right here, right now, that you're going to stand up.

The struggle is waiting for you.

The question is, are you ready?

Don't miss out!

Visit the website below and you can sign up to receive emails whenever Bradley Hall publishes a new book. There's no charge and no obligation.

https://books2read.com/r/B-A-SCSZ-REMLF

BOOKS2READ

Connecting independent readers to independent writers.